This book should be returned to any branch of the
Lancashire County Library on or before the date

2/13 NFL.
W

- 4 SEP 2018

Women in the Second World War

Women in the Second World War

Collette Drifte

First published in Great Britain in 2011 by
Remember When
An imprint of
Pen & Sword Books Ltd
47 Church Street
Barnsley
South Yorkshire
S70 2AS

ISBN 978 1 84468 096 2

Printed and bound in Great Britain
By CPI Antony Rowe, Chippenham, Wiltshire

Pen & Sword Books Ltd incorporates the Imprints of Pen & Sword Aviation,
Pen & Sword Family History, Pen & Sword Maritime, Pen & Sword Military,
Wharncliffe Local History, Pen & Sword Select, Pen & Sword Military Classics,
Leo Cooper, Remember When, Seaforth Publishing and Frontline Publishing

For a complete list of Pen & Sword titles please contact

PEN & SWORD BOOKS LIMITED
47 Church Street, Barnsley, South Yorkshire, S70 2AS, England
E-mail: enquiries@pen-and-sword.co.uk
Website: www.pen-and-sword.co.uk

Contents

Dedicated to Private W/196667 Angela Cummins, ATS, 1942 – 45

Mentioned in dispatches ...

Miss Dorothea Abbott, WLA
Private Yvette Abbott, ATS (now Mrs Yvette Wright)
Sergeant 2003451 Angela Baddeley, WAAF (now Mrs Angela Allen)
Ordinary Wren 55232 Audrey Bell, WRNS (now Mrs Audrey Parsley)
Leading Wren 53330 Margaret Carson, WRNS (now Mrs Margaret Freel)
Wren Pat Chicken, WRNS (the late Mrs Pat Straughton)
Private W/196667 Angela Cummins, ATS (now Mrs Angela Frampton)
Corporal W/121079 Joan Dargie, ATS
Leading Wren 9374 Doris Hatcher, WRNS (now Mrs Doris Lewin)
Acting Sergeant Major W/184621 Iris Holmes, ATS (now Mrs Iris
    Haddon)
Section Officer 3327 Edith Heap, WAAF (now Mrs Edith Kup)
Miss Kathleen High, WLA/Timber Corps (now Mrs Kathleen Watt)
Ordinary Wren 46632 Mary Hunter, WRNS (now Mrs Mary March)
LAC/W 2055486 Kathleen Jennings, WAAF (now Mrs Kathleen Cove)
Leading Wren 51064 Edith Keating, WRNS (now Mrs Edith Roberts)
Miss Kit Knox, WLA (now Mrs Kit Dornan)
Miss EL, VAD
Private W/21710? Peggy Mortimer, ATS (now Mrs Peggy Caudle)
Leading Wren 48444 Janet Murray, WRNS (now Mrs Janet Smith)
Miss Mabel Newton (now Mrs Mabel McCoy)
Private W/200253 Marjorie Painter, ATS (the late Mrs Marjorie Hunter)
LAC/W 470001 Jenny Parry, WAAF (now Mrs Jenny Aitchison)
Mrs VP, NFS
Lance Corporal 296285 Joan Robinson, ATS (now Mrs Joan White)
ACW 458252 Mary Rose, WAAF (now Mrs Mary Dawson)

Petty Officer MR, WRNS (the late Miss MR)
Nursing Sister ES, QAIMNS
Corporal 2071371 Sybil Scudamore, WAAF (now Mrs Sybil Singleton)
Miss Marjorie Tyson, NAAFI (now Mrs Marjorie Buzzard)
Ordinary Wren Doris Watson, WRNS
Leading Wren 375? Pamela Weightman, WRNS (now Mrs Pamela
Woodford)

I'd like to extend special thanks to Miss Dorothea Abbott, Mrs Edith Kup
and Mrs Yvette Wright, whose help and support were above and beyond
the call of duty. If there was a medal . . .

Steve Cawood, *Liverpool Daily Post & Echo*
Derek Lishman, Hexham
Steve & Lesley Middleton, Hexham
Monica Nevin, Tyneside Branch ex-WRNS Association
Andy Pryor, Riding Mill
Cathy Pugh, The Second World War Experience Centre, Leeds
John Robinson, Hexham
Susan & Mike Robinson, South Tynedale
Terry Robson, Hexham
Martin Sugarman, Archivist, AJEX Military Museum, London. For more
information about the Museum and its history, see www.ajex.org.uk
Geoff Singleton, Hexham
Derek Tiffin, Hexham
Brian Tilley, *Hexham Courant*
Margaret & Phil Walter, Allendale, Northumberland
Graham White, Northumberland
Federation of Women's Institutes: Teesside, Cumbria-Westmorland

Cumbria Life
Hexham Courant
Lady magazine
Lancashire Evening Post
Lancashire Telegraph
Liverpool Echo
Liverpool Daily Post
Newcastle Journal
North West Evening Mail
Rochdale Observer
Southport Visiter

Introduction

As a child of parents who both served in the armed forces during the Second World War, I grew up hearing the stories and anecdotes of their adventures, and I was always fascinated. Some were amusing, some were amazing and several were gruesome. As an adult, I realised the importance of documenting these stories and I promised myself that 'one day' I'd write them all down. Having read Julie Summers's fascinating book *Stranger in the House* in the spring of 2009, I decided that 'one day' had come and I really must get down to writing.

I was particularly interested in the women who went to war. What made them leave the security of hearth and home to join the massive military operation that was the Second World War? How did they cope when, coming from protected and sheltered homes, they were thrust into the rough and tumble of camp life? And what happened to them during those six dark years?

In order to find out, I sent letters to newspapers, wrote to women's organisations, magazines and clubs, contacted residential homes for the elderly, scrounged information and contact details from all my acquaintances, and then sat back to see what happened. In flooded the emails, letters, memoirs and telephone calls – wonderful ladies in their 80s and 90s, willing to tell me of their experiences; all amazing women with fascinating stories to tell.

As I travelled around the country, meeting them and speaking with them – and my goodness, what welcome hospitality awaited me in every home I visited (thank you, ladies: the tea, coffee, sandwiches and biscuits kept body and soul together!) – a pattern began to emerge. Virtually every one of them said something along the lines of, 'I've always meant to write it down, and now I'm too old, but you can do it for me while I've still got the memories fresh in my mind'. So here I am, a willing conduit, to bring you the stories these ladies have to share. Where possible, I have enabled each woman's voice to come through, by quoting her directly. Occasionally, I've added a little information or clarification so that you'll know exactly what, or who, she's talking about; or so that you'll have a better idea of the wider context of her particular anecdote. Some of the women requested anonymity, and I have respected that by changing their names and any other identifying details.

The tales cover the whole spectrum, from famous battles, such as Monte Cassino, the stuff of Hollywood and tomes discussing military strategy, to being shipwrecked by a torpedo, to simple acts of kindness, which in themselves seem nothing, but at the time meant something very special to those young women; so much so, that even 60 years on, they remember the hot water bottle tucked into a cold bed when they came in from a freezing night shift, the unexpected payment of a meal bill by a total stranger, or the loan of a locket for a special dinner date, because of the need to feel human and pretty again, and not just a clockwork soldier. The kindness of strangers, or of friends, is remembered in detail, even after the passage of so many decades.

The huge variety of services and experiences shows just how widely spread the women's contribution to the war effort was, from tilling the soil below, to servicing the engines of aircraft about to take off to the sky above, and everything in between. But something kept cropping up throughout my research almost from the word 'go'. Many times, the women mentioned the black pot-bellied stove. Even when irritated with it, because of its temperamental behaviour, the ladies spoke of it with affection. It seems to have been a symbol of cosiness, and comfort, which was often lacking when the women were on duty, 'doing a shift', 'on watch', sometimes in great danger, often in discomfort, and occasionally experiencing terror. Picture the Nissen hut where the girls slept in 'school dorm' conditions, with iron bedsteads, or bunks, in a row down each side, and no privacy. In the centre of the hut, or at each end, was the black pot bellied stove. Often, once a week, on 'domestic night', the girls had to stay in, no dates to be made for that night, no visitors, no men. Just the girls, sewing loose buttons on their tunics; darning the heels of their stockings, worn through from the constant square-bashing;

or boiling cocoa in a pan on the stove which provided warmth and a rosy glow. On other nights, girls coming off duty during the small hours crept in, careful not to wake the others. After a long and stressful shift, they would huddle around the stove to whisper, drinking their cocoa before dropping into bed, exhausted. Perhaps a fiancé had been killed; maybe a posting abroad had just come through; or a new man had been found at a dance the evening before. News, gossip, sorrows and joys were shared as the girls gathered around the stove. In our modern and conveniently-heated houses, we can't imagine the importance of that stove; but the women in this book know what it meant to them.

Seminal events such as Dunkirk or D-Day, or the Blitz, were spoken about by many of the women. Private Peggy Mortimer speaks of the soldiers as they arrived back from Dunkirk, while Corporal Joan Dargie experienced both the aftermath of Dunkirk and the build-up to D-Day. London's suffering during the Blitz has been well documented, but other cities had their share of bombs too: Portsmouth, Southampton, Coventry, Liverpool. Corporal Dargie gives her impression of Coventry[1]: 'you couldn't see a single whole building – it was awful, and yet there'd be a bit of old canvas stuck up with "Business as usual – go round the corner" [written on it]. But, my goodness, what a mess.' And Private Mortimer describes Portsmouth as she looked down at the docks receiving a plastering. She later goes on to tell of being a civilian in the London air raids. Nursing Sister ES of the Queen Alexandra Imperial Military Nursing Service describes in detail the night her ship was torpedoed, and she ended up in a lifeboat for 24 hours. All the events we've heard or read about, or have seen in cinemas, were personal experiences of these remarkable women.

By contrast, the women gave me many small pieces of information that you'll never see in the strategy books, or the historical analyses, but which nevertheless give us an insight into the 'human-interest history' of the times. For example, Lord Nuffield paid for the sanitary towels for the ATS – many of the ex-ATS women I interviewed didn't know this, only that their sanitary towels had been supplied free; or that the bomber crews of the RAF and those of the Luftwaffe had a great professional respect for each other's skill and bravery. We often fail to differentiate between the evil members of the SS and those German combatants who were fighting the war on the same terms as the Allies – not all Germans had National Socialism (Nazi) sympathies.

Sex was ever-present, even if only in the background. The women tell of the lectures they were obliged to attend, warning of the dangers of casual sex, sexually transmitted diseases and all the other 'horrors' of a promiscuous attitude. Many of the women came from sheltered homes (indeed, for some, that was the reason they joined up, as they wanted to escape what they perceived as a suffocating home life), and were unaware that other girls had a more liberal attitude to sex. So it was a shock when they discovered how some women – both civilian and in the services – used their charms to advantage. This was particularly so when the USA entered the war and the GIs hit the shores of England. The artist Beryl Cook, who was a young woman at the time, confirmed this in an interview to the BBC in the late 1970s, when she described how commodities were scarce, so the women supplemented their income by a little impromptu 'trading' with the GIs – 'we all did it'.[2] Corporal Sybil Scudamore also tells us, 'the joke was that [the GIs] would give [the girls] one silk stocking and then, when they'd had their way, they'd give them the other one'. (Not all of these liaisons were commercial transactions, however, as is shown by the thousands of marriages between US servicemen and British women, the so-called 'GI brides'.)

Wren Doris Watson smiled as she told me of the GIs' phrase 'Up with the lark, and to bed with a Wren!' 'It was [a bit naughty] but it happened quite a lot.' Everybody knows the famous, amusing phrase 'overpaid, oversexed and over here' (to which the GIs had a response: 'underpaid, undersexed and under Eisenhower'), but many a true word is spoken in jest. The phrase reflected the unease of the British men who were away from home, regarding their women; an unease that was, in many cases, justified – between 1939 and 1945, 5.3 million babies were born in the UK, of which one third were illegitimate, many born to women married to men who were away on active service.[3] Same-gender sexual activity also came as quite a shock to some of the girls. Lance Corporal Joan Robinson was perplexed when she found two ATS girls in the same bed, on her night-duty check.

The darker side of humanity is here too. There's mention of anti-Semitism, or unnecessary violence from our own troops towards civilians. A less-admirable side of the British serviceman could also come out if any of the girls danced with black soldiers, or spent time talking to them. Some of the troops would severely chastise any girl who did this – racism was clearly and shamefully present in some quarters. There was even occasional theft from girls within their own section. Thought-provoking, when you'd assume people would be considerate and thoughtful during a national crisis such as war, and the 'we all pulled together' philosophy is constantly spoken of. Clearly, some people didn't have that sense of communal, national solidarity.

Where specific facts have been mentioned, I have done all I can to check and cross-reference to ensure accuracy. But we're talking about events that took place well over 60 years ago, and memories can play tricks. If you discover anything in the text you think is inaccurate, do feel free to contact me via Pen and Sword Books, in order that I can rectify it if I'm lucky enough to go into further editions.

Finally, almost without exception, the women said, 'I enjoyed it. There were sad things, and terrible times, but for me, it was a good war, and I'm glad I was part of it'.

What more can I add?

1 Coventry suffered several small bombing raids in July and August 1940, but on the night of 14 November 1940, the city was subjected to a massive attack which virtually destroyed it. Incendiary bombs were used, as well as conventional explosives, and so fire gutted the entire city centre, as well as destroying the outlying factories, the main target of the raids.

2 See http://www.phrases.org.uk/gary-martin.html and http://www.phrases.org.uk/ meanings/oversexed-overpaid-and-over-here.html

3 See http://www.heretical.com/costello/13gleftb.html

Chapter 1

The Auxiliary Territorial Service – ATS

The women's branch of the army during the Second World War was the Auxiliary Territorial Service, or ATS. It was created in 1938 and existed until February 1949, when it became the Women's Royal Army Corps (which itself was assimilated into other corps in 1990). The ATS had its origins as a voluntary service, the Women's Auxiliary Army Corps (WAAC), formed in 1917, its members working mainly as clerks, telephonists, cooks and waitresses. This was something of a watershed since, for the first time, women offered their services in a non-nursing capacity. The WAAC was renamed the Queen Mary's Army Auxiliary Corps in 1918, but it was disbanded in 1921.

During the Second World War, apart from nurses, who joined the Queen Alexandra's Imperial Military Nursing Service (QAIMS), and medical and dental officers, who were commissioned directly into the army, all women in the army joined the ATS. The first recruits worked as clerks, cooks and storekeepers, but as the war progressed, their job opportunities were expanded to include drivers, ammunition inspectors, postal workers and orderlies. Women weren't allowed to take part in active battles, but as the shortage of men became acute, ATS girls were able to take on more demanding support roles such as radar operation, anti-aircraft guns and the military police.

By September 1941, there were 65,000 members of the ATS, and by VE Day in May 1945, some 190,000 women had joined the service. The most famous members of the ATS, and clearly they were glamorous role models who would have influenced many a girl deciding which service to opt for, were Princess Elizabeth (later Queen Elizabeth II) and Mary Churchill, the youngest daughter of Winston, the then prime minister.

In this chapter, we'll hear from ATS girls who served from the convoys in Britain to the momentous battle of Monte Cassino.

The Women

Private Yvette Abbott

Private Abbott was one of those amazingly brave women who worked on the anti-aircraft batteries, aiming to shoot down German bombers or even the bombs themselves, such as the V1s and V2s which were sent across the Channel. Posted to Portsmouth when the Blitz there was at its height, Private Abbott was exposed to danger as she and her colleagues searched for and plotted the enemy aircraft as it swooped down with its lethal payload.

I was born in London, in 1924 and I was an only child, unfortunately. I went to a boarding school for a few years at Abingdon in Berkshire, and it was after there I finished school because the war broke out. In some ways I suppose it was quite a good preparation for being away in the forces. At the beginning of the war, my mother and step-father had moved down to Devon. I was sixteen and I worked in Exeter in a dress shop and I quite enjoyed that. I really wanted to go into the Navy to become a Wren because I liked the uniform, but there was a two year waiting list, so I ended up in the army. I joined up at Honiton in Devon and was there for the start of [my] army career, where they gave you an induction course and so on, and you learnt to march.

The [other girls were] very varied; all sorts, all kinds we had. But it really taught me [about] both sides of life. I'm really quite pleased at having been in the army because that helped me enormously: I was a very shy little girl when I first went in and it brought me out. I was very quiet, didn't know anything about life whatsoever. In the army, you had to either join in or be left on the outside, so eventually I gradually learnt to become more confident with myself. I started to learn to live with people who had come from a very poor family, and with those that came from very high up. You learnt

Private Yvette Abbott, on the Isle of Wight in 1942.

to mix with the different people, and, in fact, much later on, I learnt my first lot of bad language. I had never heard bad language till I went to the army!

From Honiton, they sent you all out to different places and I was sent to Oswestry, where they built these ack–ack batteries[1] and made them up there. I learnt the instruments behind the guns – the height-finder and the predictor and plotting and so on. I was allocated to spotting at first.

The spotter used a Telescopic Identification (TI) which consisted of two sets of eye pieces at either end of a bar, which sat on top of a tripod. By looking into the eye pieces, the spotter could locate an enemy aircraft and call the range and bearing for the height-and range-finders to pinpoint and more accurately define its location. One of the great skills of the spotters was the identification of aircraft, and they had relentless training in order to ensure that they correctly spotted friend from foe.

> I hated every minute of it because you're standing in the compound behind the guns gazing up at the sky, bored out of your mind. You had to remember which was a German aircraft and which was an English aircraft, which I found very difficult anyway. But it was so boring, and I pleaded with them to let me go on something else, so they put me on the height finder for a little while. For that, you get the height of where the aircraft is above you. Then you relay [the information] to the guns through the predictor. Eventually, I landed up on a predictor which I liked mostly, and I did a little bit of plotting as well.

The height- and range-finder consisted of two telescopes in a long base tube. Different types were used, but the Barr & Stroud instrument was 18 feet long. The operators used eye pieces to look through and pinpoint the aircraft, taking height and range, and sending this to the predictor.

The predictor was an instrument used to calculate how far in front of an aircraft the gun would have to fire in order to explode close enough to the aircraft to knock it off course. Using the information from the height- and range-finder and the calculated speed, the operator would look into the eye pieces to see a small image of the aircraft. They would then turn dials to keep the image in place, and once they were 'on target', the information was automatically fed to the guns, which would then be fired.

> The predictor was a great big funny old thing. It looked a bit like a sort of Tardis really, and it had all these dials on it. You had these little handles that you had to wind quickly round to keep the needle going with the dial, because the information came into the predictor. You had to follow this very carefully, and all that information was then sent out to the guns. This was [part of the] training, and then we had to go up to a firing camp in Anglesey, right out in the wilds, to learn how to actually make the guns fire, or to help the guns to fire. We had a radio-controlled aeroplane there, which pulled this long sock behind it. We were supposed to hit the sock, and we were warned that if we hit the aeroplane, it would cost an enormous amount of money to replace it, and we very nearly hit it! We managed to get the sock once I think, but it was tremendous training. It really was; it was very good. It was left

to the men to manhandle and move the guns around; our side of it was very much less physical.

The [next] posting was down at Portsmouth and it was one of the nasty ones, because Portsmouth being a big naval port, the Germans were well after that, so we had an awful lot of raids down there. And that was quite frightening. We were right on the edge of the naval base – it was a big high bank with a rail going down, and we used to see them taking the torpedoes down to the submarines.

It was pretty noisy when those guns went off, because they were big chappies, and we didn't have any protection against the noise at all – we just put up with it. I would say we didn't have a heck of a lot of success [shooting down German planes], only occasionally. But I suppose the very fact that we were sending up shells helped to keep the Germans away a little bit, perhaps.

The raids were mostly night time but we did have some daytime ones – in fact, we had quite a few daytime ones when I think about it. One of the little Tiger Moths got hit by a German plane and he came down into our camp. It was very sad because he was a very young pilot and we could see him. He was out for the count in his cockpit and it was all aflame. We made a long line of buckets of water to try and put the thing out. One of our sergeants, he was wonderful; he got right up with an axe and axed this poor guy out of the plane. He was alive but only just. He didn't know what was going on fortunately, but as they pulled him out, his feet came away, which was very nasty. Then they took him off by ambulance, but he died on the way to hospital. Just as well I think. But it was a very sad thing, that.

The raids were horrendous. We had quite a few near-misses with bombs, sometimes when we were in the billets. And we used to hide under our beds because it was so noisy and we could hear something coming. You could hear the whistle of the bombs coming down. We didn't know where it was going to land so we sometimes got underneath our beds if we weren't near enough to the subway thing that we went underneath to. We did have an air raid shelter, but sometimes you weren't near enough it. Fortunately nobody was killed on my base. How they missed us I do not know, because we were right there by the port with searchlights going as well.

Whilst I was there, they caught a spy on our camp. There was a lot of activity going on round the guardroom. We didn't know what was going on at the time, and then we heard later that this guy came up to the camp and said could he come in and see the captain or the major or somebody. One of our very astute chappies on guardroom duty looked at him and happened to notice that the pips on his shoulders were on upside down – he had come in as an English captain. I didn't know they could be upside down, but that's what we were told. And so he thought, 'Hello, something's up here', so he reported it. All the big wigs went down and had a look, and discovered eventually that he was a German spy. So that was quite exciting. I didn't actually see him. I was longing to see him, of course. We were all longing to see him, but they bunged him straight into the prison behind the guardroom; and then he was carted away by, I suppose, Secret Service or whatever.

I was in Portsmouth for about a year, and then I went to the Isle of Wight. The raids were still going strong and we seemed to get these Stuka bombers diving down, with that scream that they used to come down with. They used to come and try to dive-bomb us while we were there, but we were just above Cowes at the time. The guns I remember that we were on were 5.5 [calibre],[2] I think it is – I was always on the big ones. Cowes was absolutely the same [as Portsmouth]. You were in Nissen huts, of course, to sleep and we had the gun emplacements and so on, so it was exactly the same, really.

We started to notice that there were a lot of flashing lights going on across a field and everybody kept saying, 'Have you seen those lights over there keep flashing away?' Our army guys went over there to try and investigate. They went very quietly, apparently, to watch, and then they discovered that there was somebody flashing lights when it was dark, when the Germans were overhead. So they called the police and also some [authority] to do with the Army, I suppose, and this guy was caught. He was a German spy who had obviously been relaying all the information, probably about our gun emplacements to his 'friends'! It was quite exciting. Of course, there was an awful lot of twittering going on, you know, and everybody was very excited about it. We thought, 'Oh gosh, we've actually got a spy on the edge of the camp'. So that was the second time I got involved – well not involved exactly, but . . .

We did have a bit of time off, though, which was allocated to us. You could have a day off a week or something, or an afternoon, or whatever it might be, depending on how much was going on. We used to go down into Cowes and go to the cinema and the fish and chip shop. That was where I met my husband actually. There was a row going on – some naval guy came out and pinched somebody else's chip as he came out of the door. My husband came round and very gentlemanly-like said, 'Oh, let me move you over here, we don't want to get you involved in the fight'. He was a sergeant in the marines and they'd come over for a big exercise. They were supposed to be taking over the Isle of Wight, you know, and we all had to be trying to stop them.

I was a private, and then on the Isle of Wight, I became a lance corporal. Well, then I blotted my copybook by coming in late twice, and so my stripes were whipped off me, and I just stayed as a private to the end of the war. I was quite happy as a private. I did ask if I could go and become an officer, but when they interviewed me they said, 'Well, we don't really think that you're ready to be officer material'. I think they were politely telling me that I definitely wouldn't become an officer!

I was there a good year and a half and then we were pushed over to Raynes Park [south-west London]. They had made this gun emplacement in the big park up there, and that was when we started to encounter the doodlebugs[3] and the horrible things that the Germans were throwing at us at the time. It was a bit late to shoot them down over Raynes Park, really, but [the authorities] were just trying hard. I mean, this was before they realised that the doodlebugs were coming in too low, and that we had to stop. I think they realised then that the guns had to be so low that we were going to be knocking people's houses – you know, the chimney pots and things off the houses. And if we got them, they'd land on the houses. There was nothing you could do. It was horrible – when they cut their engines out, you didn't know where they were going to drop. Just the other side of our camp in the road there, one came down and, in fact, we were made to go over and help the people who were in there. There was one poor little old lady who was blind and she didn't know what was happening or what had happened. It was amazing that she didn't get hurt. We couldn't believe it, but we managed to get her out and they took her away to some place for

ARMY FORM E. 511 R.

RECRUITING CENTRE
EXETER
6 JAN 1942

AUXILIARY TERRITORIAL SERVICE
NOTICE TO REPORT FOR DUTY

Date................................   Recruiting Office,

        Exeter

   I have to inform you that you are now required to report for duty in the Auxiliary Territorial Service.

   I am therefore to request that you will report to the Officer Commanding *No 3 ATS TC. Heathfield Camp — Harlie.* on *Friday 23-1-42.* A railway ~~bus~~ warrant for your journey is enclosed herewith.

   You should report as early in the day as possible. *by 2 pm.*

            Pat Brooke 4/c
            Recruiting Officer.

Wt. 42041/414 50,000 1/40 KJL/40 **Gp. 698/3** Forms E 511 R/1
Wt. 11121/225 100M 5/41 KJL/5226/8 **Gp. 698/3**   **P.T.O.**

The call-up paper for Private Yvette Abbott (front and reverse). Note the list of 'must-have' items!

CLOTHING. 2 pairs of pyjamas or nightgowns are essential.

You will be issued with a complete uniform and necessaries on arrival at the Depot, but the following would be useful if you wish to bring them with you:

 1 Woollen cardigan.   ~~1 Towel.~~
 1 Tooth brush.   ~~1 Sponge or equivalent.~~
 1 Housewife, with buttons, needles 6 Handkerchiefs.
  and thread.   ~~1 pair gym. shoes.~~
 1 Complete set of underclothing,
  including 1 pair knickers. *Iwam shut*

GENERAL INSTRUCTIONS *or strong shoes*

Bring your
 (a) National Registration Book. (b) Ration Book. (c) Civilian Gas Respirator.

If your Health Insurance Contribution Card and/or Unemployment Book are in the possession of your employer or of the Employment Exchange, you should obtain them, if possible, and bring them with you. But IF YOU ARE UNABLE TO GET THEM YOU MUST NOT DELAY JOINING ON THIS ACCOUNT. If you have to apply to the Employment Exchange for your Unemployment Book, you should take with you the Receipt Card (U.I.40) and this notice.

If your Unemployment Book is with the Exchange and you cannot get it, you should bring the Receipt Card with you instead and hand it in on joining.

them to look after her. And poor souls, some of them were killed; the houses were just smashed to pieces. It was dreadful really. By then, the conventional raids had more or less ceased and it wasn't so bad then. So apart from trying to hit the V1s, which was difficult anyhow, there wasn't so much for you to do. That's why they decided to put some of the ack-ack batteries down out into Kent to catch the bombs before they came in. But we didn't get the chance and we all got split up into different places, which we were all very unhappy about.

I was sent up to the Pay Corps in Leeds, which was horrifying. But again it was another experience. It was quite different because it was almost like being in an office. Well, we were in an office. We were actually put in an old boot factory and we were given these enormous ledgers to count up, to add up the pages, each page. We were supposed to do one ledger a day. I couldn't even get through half a ledger, not even a quarter of the ledger, because I wasn't very good at adding up and so I was always being told off for that! But we had some fun.

When we were in Raynes Park, we put on a big NAAFI show and we needed to get some costumes for this thing. My step father was in the film business at the time, and he got us into the Shepperton where they had a huge wardrobe. So we all went up and, while we were there, somebody came in and said, 'Oh we're looking for someone. We're doing a big hype on this studio trying to display it to everybody and let them know what's going on here. The person with the nearest measurements to a film star will be the one that will get the job', and I got it!

I was with Phyllis Calvert[4], and so I had to go up again.

She'd been in a film called *Madonna of the Seven Moons*, and they had all the gowns that she wore. I had to put these gowns on and they took photographs for this promotion that they were doing for the wardrobes. Then [Phyllis Calvert and I] had tea together. She was an absolutely charming lady; she was wonderful.

They also took one photograph of me in very pretty cami-knickers, which were emerald green and black. They said they were going to put it in the paper, and I thought, 'I hope they don't'. But, of course, it was that one that came out in the paper. So you can imagine the boys the next day – all the wolf whistles and all the rest of it. It was so embarrassing! So that was that.

There were many benefits from my war service. Although war is a terrible thing, I benefited from it, I really did. I was very lucky.

This interview was adapted and reproduced with the permission of the Second World War Experience Centre, Leeds, and of Mrs Yvette Wright.

Private W/196667 Angela Cummins

Private Angela Cummins was an Irish volunteer who joined the ATS in January 1943 at the age of 21. She was trained as a clerk, being based in Belfast initially, before a posting to London. After volunteering for active service abroad, Angela was sent to the Allied Forces Headquarters in the Royal Palace at Caserta, some 17 miles from Naples in Italy. She arrived there as the battle for Monte Cassino[5] was raging in 1944. Angela was seconded to the Americans, working in Censorship, in the intelligence section.

> I was based at the Royal Palace, Caserta, from 1944 to 1946. I volunteered to go abroad on active service – we weren't conscripted or sent; we volunteered to go, because for each girl who volunteered to go, a man was released for duty at the front. That's how they got us to go out there, and that's why I volunteered. I was called to go to London – at lunchtime I got a tap on the shoulder and was told, 'Go home on embarkation leave. We're sending you abroad'. When I came back, they put me on a train to Scotland and from there I sailed on the *Queen of Bermuda*. I remember when we docked at Naples, I was shocked. The quayside was seething with people: servicemen from all over the world, and civilians, begging. They were mainly old people, women and children. I was shocked at their appearance – they looked starved, and they were dressed in rags. Many of them didn't have proper shoes on. Instead they had on their feet a bit of wood with a strip of cloth across the instep that had been nailed into the wood at each side. I'd never seen anything like it. I was coming down the gangplank when I saw a heavily-pregnant young woman approach a Tommy, with her hand held out, begging. He was just ahead of me, going down the gangplank as well, and when he got to just a bit above her, he raised his boot and kicked her with full force into her stomach. I remember feeling sick to my soul as she fell back with the force of it, and curled up in a ball, obviously in terrible pain. I often wonder what happened to her – she must surely have lost that baby; maybe she even died herself. Terrible.
>
> I ended up at the Royal Palace which was the Allied Forces Headquarters, and there were all sorts of nationalities there, all sorts of uniforms; some of them looked so gorgeous compared with the khaki that ours were made of. I was sent to work with the

Americans as a clerk for Allied Intelligence, in Censorship. I had to take an oath of secrecy, as a lot of stuff passed through my hands. In my office, there was just me and an ATS officer who was a linguist. They used to bring in the captured German mail by the sack load and just tip it out on the floor of the office. She used to translate it and pick out useful pieces of information and I had to type it all out, making so many copies to send out to different people. We were run ragged, starting work at 7 o'clock in the morning and it was often 9 o'clock at night before you could go back to the billet. If you were lucky, you might find a bit of time at midday to get something to eat.

Another part of my job was preparing the travel passes for people who were going all over the world, obviously on various missions. One day, just as I was about to go for something to eat, a chap came in and asked me to do his travel documents for Rio de Janeiro. I was hot and tired and on my own – everybody else had gone to lunch, so I just told this chap he'd have to come back in the afternoon and get it done then. Well, he sweet-talked me into doing his documents and off he went. I was miffed because by then I'd missed my lift to the canteen. When the sergeant came back after lunch and checked my work tray, he gave me a tongue-lashing for doing this chap's documents, ranting on and on that he should've done it, not me. To cut a long story short, it turned out that the chap was George Lascelles, the future Earl of Harewood and cousin of the Queen. Being Irish and without a clue about who was who in the royal family, the name meant nothing at all to me – he was just a chap who made me late for my lunch! But, do you know, he was so down-to-earth, no airs and graces, you'd never have known his background. But that was the amazing thing about the war – you met all sorts, from all walks of life; it was a real melting pot.

Once a week, the Colonel planned a trip to somewhere nice and he'd take the whole lot of us out. If we were going somewhere like the theatre we'd have to pay for our own tickets though. We often went to the opera at the San Carlo in Naples and we even saw Gigli[6] – things like that we were able to do. We had some beautiful experiences.

In April [1945], I was sent to Bari, with my friend, to relieve them in the offices. There was an outbreak of measles among the girls and they were too poorly to work. We were there for a couple of weeks,

I think. Anyway, one day, we were going back to our billet after work, and we were walking down this road, hot and dusty as usual. Suddenly, there was an almighty explosion that just shook the ground under our feet and seemed to reverberate on and on, boom after boom. We threw ourselves onto the ground, curled up and trying to get close into the walls of the buildings, thinking there was an air raid or something. As I looked up, I saw what I thought was a football rolling, almost bouncing, down the centre of the road, before it came to rest in the gutter. When we stood up and I had a closer look, I realised it was a man's head, taken clean off his body. I have no idea where the torso was. I was almost sick, I can tell you. The explosion turned out to have been an ammunition ship in the harbour, which had blown up. The loss of life and the damage was awful.[7]

During the battle at Cassino, you could hear it from where we were – thump, thump, thump – which was actually the bombing of Cassino. It was a continual thudding and you wanted it to stop, just for a minute, to give you a rest. It was an awful noise that you can't describe and you never forget. You feel as if everything's shattering around you. When the troops moved out and continued on the road to Rome, the battle site had to be checked. Colonel Finn called us all together and we started out in cars, to go up to see what state the place was in after the bombardment, and to make sure all the Germans had been flushed out. As we got onto the road leading up there, we had to get out of the cars because the road was just pitted with craters. But you couldn't walk very easily either, so I decided to walk on the wall instead. It was a loose stone wall with flat pieces along the top and as I was walking, we heard all this screaming and shouting from the top, from above us on the mountain. It was Polish soldiers who'd seen me on the wall and were screaming, 'Get off the wall – it's mined!' The Germans had taken out a flat stone out every so often and put a mine in because they knew that our soldiers would be climbing up the mountain. By rights I should've been blown sky high, but it wasn't my time, that day, was it?

As we stood looking around, we saw a light above us, flashing every so often. Colonel Finn shouted us to get flat on the ground, and that we had to get out of there somehow or we'd be shot. Some of the group went up to investigate and it turned out to be a wardrobe hanging in an L-shape corner of a building that had been bombed. The wardrobe door was going back and forth in the breeze and the 'flashlight' was actually the sun catching on the mirror: that's what we could see and we thought was it Germans signalling!

As we were climbing to the top, all the way we saw Polish soldiers, clearing up after the battle, collecting bodies. I saw a bayonet sticking out from behind a rock and decided to have it for a souvenir. I went over and gave it a tug, and out rolled a German body. I was shocked, I can tell you! I didn't take the bayonet, after all, as you can imagine. When we did get up to the top, we walked to the edge and looked down, and you just couldn't believe it. The whole plain was a mass of lakes where there were bomb craters that had filled up with water, and everything was just flattened. The monastery was a mess – it had been bombed from the air and it was just jagged walls; it was nothing but a hill of stones.

As we were up there picking through the rubble, I picked up a very small piece of fresco. It sat in the palm of my hand and it had the face of the Virgin Mary on it. I thought, 'I'm going to keep this', and then suddenly I got smacked on the back of my hand. This monk had come out of a hole in the ground – they'd all gone down into the cellars to shelter – and he'd knocked the piece out of my hand. He said to me that they were going to rebuild the monastery and that they wanted every piece of the original they could find; if each one of us took a souvenir, there'd be nothing left to use.

My office was in the throne room in the palace and they'd partitioned it into sections with wooden screens. My desk was beside the main doors and one morning, some time after the battle was over, I heard a lot of noise in the hallway outside, and I wondered what was going on. I was frightened as I thought the Germans had beaten the Allies back and had come into the HQ. I stood there waiting and suddenly all the top brass came through the doors, Germans as well as ours. They marched down the length of the throne room [which was Angela's 'office'] and went into the room next door, to sign the treaty of surrender.[8] We didn't know what was going on, but we found out afterwards. It's a funny thing, but we didn't think anything much of it at the time, but when I look back now and realise the importance of the whole thing, and think that I was there as history was being made, it's just amazing.

Corporal W/121079 Joan Dargie

Corporal Joan Dargie, who was born in 1923, joined the ATS in 1942 and served until 1946. She was a convoy driver and qualified as a Second Class Mechanic. When she left her native Northumberland, she was posted to the very grand surroundings of Attingham Hall, the seat of Lord Berwick, near Shrewsbury.

> I did one term at a teacher's training college which had been evacuated from Liverpool to Bingley [Yorkshire], and I came back on holiday for Christmas, and I just went off and joined up without telling the family. I got so tired of school, I joined up and I was sent

to Dalkeith [Scotland] to do my initial training. Because I'd been at boarding school off and on, it was a shock to my system, to suddenly find myself in a Nissen hut full of women who were a lot older than I was, crying their eyes out because they'd never been away from home before. There were actually about three of us in that hut of 24 women who had been away from home, and we tried to entertain and cheer up all these other girls – I can remember putting our tin hats underneath our jackets, and absolutely fooling around. [The training] was learning how to take orders, and marching around the streets, and generally learning what the army was all about.

The first things I sent home for were a toothcomb and a roll of toilet paper. And a bath plug, because if you went for a bath, the plugs were always missing – people pinched them! You got frightfully annoyed – you'd use your flannel to try and stop the water flowing out. And the toothcomb was because there were a lot of head lice around. My poor mother wondered what on earth I was going to ask for next! For the first week we weren't allowed out at all, and then, when we were allowed into the town, I can remember two or three of us going into a hotel in Dalkeith and asking if we could have baths. You couldn't have a bath very often because there were too many girls and not enough baths, and right through my army career I found that.

Initial training was only for a month and then we all dispersed. Then you had to decide what you wanted to do, and I opted to be a convoy driver, so I was sent to a place called Gresford, in north Wales, near Wrexham. I did a basic training of driving, starting in a 15cwt truck, and after my basic training I was sent to Shrewsbury, and I was there for four years.

I went to live in Attingham Hall which belonged to Lord Berwick, but it had been taken over for the army. It had large grounds where you could keep all the vehicles and they were called Vehicle Reception Depots. Part of our driving would be to go to Birmingham, Wolverhampton, Coventry or wherever, to collect vehicles from the factory, and take them to any Vehicle Reception Depot – it might be your own; it might be others. The other task was to collect vehicles from Reception Depots and take them to wherever they were needed. Maybe it was just to some Company, or maybe they were ready for shipping. We used to go to Glasgow, to Edinburgh and Leith, London docks a lot, Liverpool, Manchester where they were nearly always boxed into crates. We'd then go back by train. Some of the girls used to write little notes and hide them [in the vehicles] and we did get some very interesting letters back from time to time. One of my friends corresponded with a boy who was out in India and he wrote the most wonderful letters – very descriptive, without having to let on where he was, for safety.

In fact, I got into trouble once. It was a convoy to London and I was in charge. The person in charge of a convoy was at the back so that if anybody broke down, you were there to look after them. Somebody with reasonable intelligence had to lead because there weren't any signposts – you had to do it all by map reading or by stopping and asking. Well, one of the girls broke down, not very far out from Shrewsbury. I just could not get her vehicle started and we had to abandon it in the end. We battled on and eventually reached the docks in London, but the convoy wasn't there – no trucks around, so we found somebody to ask, and they said, 'Oh that lot have been put on the ship already'. They told us where to go to have ours put onto the ship and I had to tell them we'd got one truck missing. They said it didn't matter that one truck was missing because they weren't sailing for another fortnight. When I reported back that it didn't matter about the truck, because the ship wasn't sailing for another fortnight, I didn't half get a rocket. You weren't supposed to mention that sort of thing – when a ship was sailing! No. 'Careless Talk Costs Lives' was the slogan.

Sometimes we'd go on convoy maybe three times a week to London. We got a subsistence allowance – can't remember how much it was; but I think if we were on a day trip it was 1/6d and that got your lunch and things like that. If we went to London, we stayed in Gower Street. I can remember we went down on a Monday and we all went out that night to Soho and had a nice Chinese [meal]; back on a Tuesday; down again on the Wednesday – Lyon's Corner House[9]; home again on the Thursday; back down to London on the Friday and it was a bun in Hyde Park this time!

After Dunkirk, a lot of the vehicles they'd managed to rescue and bring back were waterlogged and not fit [for service]. We used to have to go and get them and take them to places where they'd have to be repaired. I can remember driving around Bristol and I think we were four, all of us tied together, towing – an awful lot of towing went on! – and I was at the back. I was swinging out and I really couldn't control it! There were the silly things like having to drive with no lights. Somewhere in the middle of Bristol there was a statue of Neptune and there were red lights all around it so you didn't drive into it. So we pinched them and put them on the back of our truck. The other good trick, if you didn't have a rear light, was a slice of beetroot in a torch – if you sliced it thinly enough, it gave a good red light through. We got up to all sorts of improvisations.

We drove all sorts of vehicles. The American ones were often difficult to get used to because they had the clutch and the accelerator in the opposite place to where you were used to. And the Jeeps! The Ford Jeeps were alright, but the Willy Jeeps had a windscreen wiper which you had to work with your hand. Now you try steering with one hand and working the windscreen wiper with the other – it's like patting your head and rubbing your chest!

Coropral Joan Dargie and colleagues on the way to Glasgow with their convoy.

And great big Portees[10] – oh, we always used to get them in the winter. All they had was a little square as a windscreen, and you were absolutely perished. I can remember sitting on one hand to get it warm, then sitting on the other. We were frozen – your face was frozen, and your nose. Fog and frost – ughhh! And then in the summer, you were driving one of these Bedford trucks which had the engine in the cab beside you, and you were rolling up your trousers because of the heat.

I got ten shillings a week when I first went in, and you had to buy things like soap, and general things. Now, one very interesting thing was that Lord Nuffield supplied the ATS with sanitary towels for free. Wasn't that a thoughtful thing to do? I know, though, that some of them were wasted – one of our girls used to make soft toys and she used them for the stuffing. Better not tell Lord Nuffield that!

I had my 21st birthday at Attingham Hall and the Sergeants' Mess sent me a crate of beer and my mother managed to get a wonderful cake to me, made at a lovely cake shop in Morpeth [Northumberland] and they'd all given sugar and goodness knows what, to make it. I promised I'd bring a little bit of the cake home on my next leave, so I saved a bit of it. Coming home on leave, we were in a carriage with a whole lot of sailors going home on leave as well, and at one of the stations the train stopped. The sailors said, 'You girls want a cup of tea?', so they went off and got us cups of tea. Well, one of them said, 'Gosh, I could just do with a bit of cake', so I got my piece of cake out! So my mother didn't get any of my cake in the end!

On the build-up to D-Day – which, of course, we didn't know about at the time – all leave was cancelled. We were doing nothing but drive south; all the vehicles were going to Weymouth. We thought there was something going on, with all these vehicles being shifted south instead of going to the docks. At a place called Yattenden [Berkshire], there were Americans, and some British, and they knew they were getting ready for embarkation. I don't think they knew exactly where they were going, though. We had a wonderful night with them, and I've often wondered how many of them were left the next week, you know. We had a party, and I think we all got up and did a party piece, or sang, and they were all so cheerful, those men.

Corporal Dargie was in London as the V J Day celebrations were getting into full swing. 15 August 1945 was the day Japan surrendered and became known as V J Day –Victory over Japan Day. Thousands of people spilled into Trafalgar Square to celebrate the end of the war, and Joan was there to witness it first-hand. Indeed, she couldn't avoid being swept up by the joy. Here's an extract from a letter she wrote to her mother that day:

Attingham Hall,
Uffington,
15th August 1945

Dear Mummy,

Well, it is over at last, but not for me until I'm out of the army! There are very wild rumours going around that the girls will be out by Xmas but I'm still sticking to Easter. For a Victory day, today has been somewhat queer as we have been on the road all day! Yes, we were in London last night and did so wish that we could stay down. However we had a very interesting time. We went to see 'Mr Skeffington' [starring Bette Davis and Claude Rains], a very good picture, then wandered down to Piccadilly. Once there, there was no getting away. Crowds of people milling around, rockets and squibs flying all over the place. We bought hats and rattles and joined the crowd!

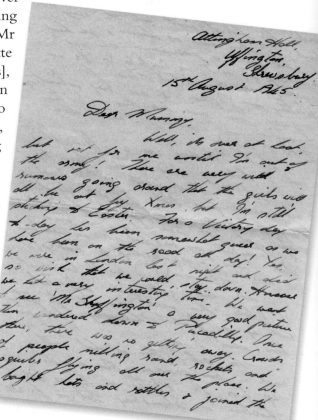

Part of a letter from Corporal Joan Dargie, dated 15 August 1945, describing the V J Day celebrations.

We had to walk all the way back as there were no buses and we had a word with a policeman who was standing on duty in Oxford Street. He was guarding an Exhibition Piece for Victory over Japan and was very interesting. Anyway you will hear him on *In Town Tonight*[11] next Saturday. He is also going to sing! . . .

Acting Sergeant Major W/184621 Iris Holmes

Iris Holmes was 18 at the beginning of the war and she and her mother did a First Aid course in Croydon, because she felt she ought to do something. Before joining the ATS, she also became involved with the Air Raid Precautions (ARP) in her local area.

> We were on fire patrol, watching for the incendiary bombs. Each house had to alternate with your neighbours: they did 10.00pm till midnight or something, and you did midnight till 2.00am, and somebody else did 2.00am – 4.00am. You had to be awake and watch out, if there was a raid on, for incendiaries. The [bombs] showered a lot of them out, so they started little fires in all sorts of places, but they were heavy enough to come through the roof of your house. That would set your loft on fire at least, but if you got a shovel or two of sand on them, they would have gone out.
>
> When I was 21 I was called up and I was passed as A1 fit. I went to a training centre in Guildford. You were given a metal mug and a knife, fork and spoon; they were yours and you had to keep them, and put your name on them. Then they formed you up into three ranks and you went to the stores, where you were given a kit bag. In the kit bag you had four shirts and eight collars, [some] pairs of khaki slacks, stockings, one pair of brown leather shoes, one pair of plimsolls, one PE top, one pair of brown divided-skirt shorts, three or four vests, two or three bras, two or three best-type material knickers, and three pairs of what they called 'khaki issue' knickers which were silky, khaki in colour with elastic round the bottoms. We soon put those up out of the way! You had to mark it all with your number [and your rank and name]. You did it in Indian ink because it wouldn't wash out. You had to have Silvo and polish the buttons on your uniform; and you had to have boot polish, and polish your shoes every day, and underneath too.
>
> Then you had to go and be medically examined, so you went into a corridor where you had to strip. Some of the girls had never

stripped in front of each other before, but you had to do it, so you didn't make too much fuss about it, and carried on. But some were trying to hold things [in front of them] and not get exposed before they got something off! There was one girl who must've worn her vest for six months without it being washed – it was really grubby and all matted up; it was horrid. But some people were very dignified, and had nice pretty underwear. After that, we had to go and sit on a chair, and the nurse looked at your head. Some of the girls were directed to the left, and I was directed to the right. I thought, 'Oh dear, I'm the only one over here. What's the matter with me?' But I was the only one who hadn't got nits out of that group! Others joined me eventually, though.

They marched you, and we did drill every day. You did route marches, and after a route march, they came down and looked at your feet to see how many blisters you'd got, because they were heavy shoes. We had to learn the discipline and we had lectures on different things. Every day you had to fall in and march so you'd gradually improve and you knew what to do after a few days.

After you'd been there about three weeks, you had an interview with the officer in charge and you had to do a selection test. I did the whole thing because to me it was a piece of cake. Before you were dispatched, they worked out what you could do, and I was sent to do an office job. Then they were building up gun sites so I was sent to the Aldershot area, where I met up with a whole lot of new people, men and girls. I was in the office which was reasonably cushy. When I'd done a month there, I was sent to a [gun] site in Kent, near Chatham, so I wasn't that far from home. It was 64 Battery. You got a 24-hour pass once a week, and every so often, you got a seven-day leave. We were really lucky: the railway was always alright between Chatham and Bromley; I used to get a train to Bromley and then a bus home. So when I'd had my day's leave, Mum used to come with me to Bromley when I was going back. There was a little place where you could get a cup of tea and a bun or something; so we used to have tea and a bun, or whatever they'd managed to rake up in the way of cakes. Then I'd get a [train] to go back, and Mum would go home on the bus.

Where I was, they were heavy guns, four-fives anti-aircraft. They had what was called colours and letters of the day. The commanding officer had a list of all the secret stuff and he knew [which] British fighters [were] up. If you had the ground staff going to fire on things, you had to have the colours and letters of the day so you didn't shoot at English planes. The guns were very, very loud.

Being office staff, we weren't with the operational girls; we were in different Nissen huts from [them]. You had to be in bed by 23.59 hrs; also, the officers would come round to make sure you were all in. In the summer, we were up at 6.00am, and in the winter it was 6.30am. If you wanted a bath, you had to be careful because there was only so much hot water. When my friend Sheila would come off duty in the morning, she'd go and run a hot bath; and when she'd had a bath, she'd run it again, and come and wake me up and say, 'The water's running for a bath', so I'd get up, and somebody else would be ready to go after me. But by that time, the water had all run out and it was cold. There was a line around the bath because you were only allowed so much water.

When you had your meals, you couldn't be posh and have a dessert spoon and fork; you had your knife, fork and spoon, and that was your lot. When you came out of the dining hall, you had to wash your knife, fork and spoon in a big trough, along with everybody else's – it's the silly things like that you suddenly remember! The food was adequate, but plain. You had a cooked breakfast, but you didn't always have an egg; you'd have bacon with something. You had fried-up potatoes quite often. You didn't have toast and marmalade. There was a dish full of margarine.

There were some girls called height-finders, and others called predictors. Some of them worked out which [direction the enemy aircraft] was coming from and how fast it was going, so that at a given time, as it came over your air space to where it should be, it was time to fire [the guns].

The officers could [go] to the village to have a pint in the local, and the idea was the [gun site] could phone up the pub if an alert came on, and the officers would have to go back quickly! The Honourable Humphrey Stewart was [there] one night, and he came in the next day with brambles scored all over him. The road went round a corner, and he'd landed up in a hedge, off the army bike [in the hurry to get back]!

I was with them nearly the whole of my career, until the war had pretty well ended, and then the gun sites were dismissed. I was the only ATS girl who went to Morton Morrell, near Leamington Spa, to a beautiful ancestral house. Then some more girls joined me, and I was the only officer, so I was in charge of these girls, because I was a corporal. Then they put me up to sergeant, and I was now about 23 or 24. I could [still] get home all right. You'd get off duty on Friday evening (but I had to be back by Sunday) because the office didn't work to full strength over the weekend, so I'd often get the weekend to come home.

Everywhere had white bits painted on – the trees and the kerbstones, so you could get about in the dark. You heard bombs coming down, that made a whistling noise, then this terrific crump, and you thought it sounded as if it was this way or that way, and you might know roughly which road you thought it had landed in. It was only when you got up in the morning and you looked along that you started seeing that some of the houses had got a bit of damage; and it gradually got worse as you went along, or the other side of the road. On the radio, you got things like, 'In the air raid over London yesterday morning, a large number of German aircraft came over. We shot down seven German aircraft but without any loss to ourselves'. You got a daily [report] like that. You would go to the cinema and then if there was an air raid, they would flash it up on the screen, 'There's an air raid warning', and you could get up and leave if you wanted to. In the big theatre in Croydon, people stayed in [once] because there was a good film on, and a lot of them were killed.

I once bought some nylons on the cheap at Croydon market. All they wanted were your clothing coupons, really. They said you could have three pairs of nylons for two coupons. When you got them home, there'd be the seam all the way down the front or they'd only got half a leg – they were terrible; absolute malfunction by whoever had made them. You couldn't wear them at all – not even two you could wear! I was so annoyed, I went back down to the market straight away, but they'd gone.

The above interview was kindly conducted by Dr Steve Middleton.

Private W/21710, Peggy Mortimer

Private Peggy Mortimer came from Wiltshire. After leaving school at 14, she eventually trained as a waitress, which is the skill she took with her into the ATS when she joined up in 1939.

My sister said to me, when the war began, 'Shall we go and enlist?' and I said, 'I don't think Mother would like that'. 'Well, we won't tell her' till we've done it,' she said. Which we did – [Mother] hit the roof! In time, an officer came to see us, because they were trying to get women for certain jobs, to release the men to go to the front. Well, I wasn't 18 until December (this was September), but there was one way she could get me in. After we did our [initial] training for so many weeks, we were heading for Portsmouth, and I'd have to be [the officer's] batwoman[12] until I was 18. We went to the Royal

Engineers in Portsmouth, where we were billeted in the married quarters, but the [wives] were no longer there because of the war. So [the officer] and I were in the end house, and I looked after her, until I was old enough to do a proper job. Then I joined my sister in the Officers' Mess, where she was a cook, and I waited on the officers at table. From there I went to the Sergeants' Mess, which I liked better.

Private Mortimer told how her future husband returned from the Dunkirk beaches with only the clothes he was dressed in, and shocking tales of men losing their minds, as they were sitting targets for the

Germans. Private Mortimer herself was in Portsmouth at the time, working in the Sergeants' Mess.

> We were confined and not allowed out, so we knew something was going on. We were overwhelmed by chaps coming back. First of all, a load of them would come in; then there'd be two or three more coming in from wherever they'd been. They'd just come wandering in, to whichever camp was handy for them. They had come home on the boats and were just dropped off somewhere, so they'd just come wandering in; and we had to feed them and look after them.

Private Mortimer was in Portsmouth, too, when the docks were bombed.[13]

> We even had a bomb at the end of the fort where we were actually living at the time. [During the raids] we had a bird's eye view, because we were on the top of the hill, and Portsmouth was down [below]. It started quite slowly. Every night they came and bombed the docks. It was like the whole world was on fire. It was absolutely ghastly. But then, of course, it went quiet finally. Behind the fort there were caverns, with walkways, and we all had to go down there [for shelter]. There were beds, and several times it happened that we had to go and spend the night down there. They thought we were being invaded, so each time something happened, off we went down.
>
> Then, after that, we were all sent up to North Wales, both the men and the women, to Wynnstay Hall,[14] where we had Nissen huts in the grounds. Out of the blue I was offered [the chance] to go on a cookery course, which I did – I went to Hereford, and did a six-week course. It meant more money and more status. So I went back to the Sergeants' Mess, but this time I was cooking. I enjoyed that; it was really good. It was interesting and you met a lot of people, as they came and went. There was never any shortage of food – you just sent an order in and it came; we got everything. I finished up in charge of the Sergeants' Mess. That's how I met my husband. I've always had a [good singing] voice, so I was doing the concerts on a Sunday night. The chap who normally accompanied me on the piano was away this particular week, and Sergeant Caudle took over – that was fine, as I had met him a few times. He taught me a few

new things and we got together (and we made music for many years after that!).

Private Mortimer married Sergeant Gerry Caudle, who by now had been posted to Watford, and after their honeymoon in London, they had to separate and return to their respective bases. Peggy finally went to Watford when her husband managed to have her transferred. She left the ATS in 1943, because she was having a baby. She went to London, to live with her mother-in-law, and there she experienced the Blitz at its full force.

> The worst part of the war for me was living with my child through all the bombing in London. The first year of my son's life he spent in the shelter, practically! It was 1944, and there were doodlebugs and rockets. It was pretty grim – you never knew whether your house was going to be there in the morning. In the daytime, you did the things you'd normally do – clean the house, go shopping, that sort of thing. Shopping was difficult – fruit was almost non-existent. I got one [ration book] for me and one for the child, but food was difficult to get.
>
> There were seldom daytime raids until the doodlebugs came. They were noisy, but you welcomed the noise because as soon as the noise stopped, the thing dropped, and you thought, 'Well, it's gone past me, so it won't be here'. Then the rockets came. Well, you didn't know when they were coming – there was no warning at all; they just dropped, so it was pretty bad. In the night, it used to be dreadful. I used to put my baby to bed in the shelter. It was an Anderson shelter[15] in the garden – everybody had [them]. We shared one with the neighbours. We had beds and a cooker, and lights – everything we needed. They made it like home, really. So every night at [my son's] bedtime, I would take him and I'd go to the shelter, in my pyjamas, ready for bed. You'd hear the sirens and the bumps and you'd wonder 'Are all the windows intact?' It was pretty grim.

Yet, despite the difficulties, Peggy found much about the war a positive experience.

> I enjoyed the whole thing, really. I enjoyed my time in the forces. I met good people, bad people, indifferent people. On the whole, I enjoyed it – I wouldn't have missed it for anything.

Private W/200253 Marjorie Painter

Marjorie Painter was working for a firm of accountants in Stockport, Manchester, before she joined up in July 1942. She was only 17 years old and, while her father was willing to let her go, her mother was none too happy. She trained for signals in the ATS.

I'd more or less just started work, about a year before I joined up. First I was posted to Lancaster to do my square bashing and get my uniform – that was for six weeks. I quite enjoyed it but we weren't allowed any freedom; we didn't go out at all; we had to stay in barracks for the whole six weeks of the initial training. We used to parade on the parade ground and then we used to go on marches in Lancaster. It was up and down hill, but we got through it! We had

all our jabs and then I moved to Queensbury in Bradford to do six weeks' training to do teleprinting[16] and so on. It was August and it was bitterly cold; I got chilblains while I was there!

A lot of the girls were crying; they were homesick. It really upset some of them, as they'd never been away from home. I felt sorry for them really. Some hadn't got much money. I was very fortunate. I know it was only ten bob a week to start with, but my father always gave me a £20 note to do me for three months; the big white £20 notes. And about a week before I was due my leave, we used to have a bender! And I got donations from various institutions he used to belong to, so I wasn't really short of money. There was one rule in the crowd I knocked about with: we did not lend money. So, if they were skint, and we were going to the cinema or somewhere, we'd take them with us and pay for them. Then, when they were flush, they'd do it for someone else. That way, you kept your friends. But it wasn't very often that they were flush because a lot of them had to send money home, because the breadwinner had gone [to war]. Some of them had to tip up half their wages, which wasn't much anyway.

I could get home from Bradford on a Sunday. I used to walk to Halifax to get the train to Stockport at about 4 o'clock in the morning, so I was always home for Sunday lunch; and my mother used to do my washing and anything else I wanted done, and I got back for Sunday evening. I didn't mind; it was nice just to go home for a few hours.

I did my six weeks and I passed out all right, and then they sent me to Middleton just outside Manchester. I had to go into private billets because there was no command or anything there, just a small unit of signals, and that was all really. I wasn't there long when they asked for volunteers to go to the Isle of Man, so I put my name down. We went in December, just before Christmas 1942, and I was there until January 1944. It was hard work but I enjoyed it. I was on teleprinters and we were down in the cellars of a big house; I think they'd been the kitchen at one time. The cellars were reinforced and fitted out in case you got a bomb. You went down the cellar steps and there were two teleprinters which were like glorified computers, two chairs and a sofa, that's all. If you did a night duty, you went on at 10.00pm until 8.00am. There were two men – from signals – who did the ordinary phones, the switchboard, so we had company, but there were always two of us on [duty]. We used to take our shoes off because our feet swelled at night when we were on duty, and in the morning we had to empty our shoes because they were full of cockroaches! We weren't terribly busy because it was only a small station, and we never got bombed at the Isle of Man.

I liked it there – we had some nice times. In the summer we used to go swimming. There was a lovely beach. We used to come off duty at say 1 o'clock and we'd go and have a swim, then get something to eat; and go back on duty later on perhaps. We were billeted by the Villa Marina just off the Promenade, with an Irish landlady, and for breakfast, you got everything bar the kitchen sink: bacon, egg, homemade potato cakes, sausages. She had a friend who had a farm, and they really weren't rationed on the Isle of Man. She fed us well and I put on quite a lot of weight!

There were Italian prisoners at Douglas on one side of the island, and they just had wire mesh round the hotels which had been commandeered. They were quite happy – they used to sit on the hotel steps and play their guitars and musical instruments as you were going past. You couldn't help but smile at them. But on the other side were the German prisoners or anybody that was a serious [threat], at Port St Mary's.[17] I had a friend who used to go round the camps with films. She had a driver and he took us round and showed the films to the troops. But we weren't allowed in Port St Mary's otherwise. There were other camps with ack-ack guns as well and she used to go round showing these films, so if I was off duty, I'd go with her. Sometimes we used to go for a drink, and there were some very nice forces clubs. Woolworths in the centre of the town was taken over by the Salvation Army, and on Sunday morning we always used to go there and have a cup of tea and a biscuit, or whatever they'd got. There was also [a place] where we used to go and get egg and chips at night! There was a cinema, and the Villa Marina used to put on a concert on a Sunday night, because everywhere was shut down on Sundays – no cinemas or dance halls were open; and the pubs were all shut. At the Villa Marina there'd be variety shows sometimes, or some entertainers used to come over, singers and dancers, and anybody they could get hold of.

I got visitors there. My father always used to come and see me because he liked the Isle of Man; he used to go to the TT races when they were on. And friends I used to work with used to come over and see me.

Then I got posted to Chester, to the north-west command base. It was a big building that housed all sorts of things. We were billeted in a theological college that had been requisitioned for the army. It was nice because those who worked shifts got our own cubicle. Those who were doing other things had to go downstairs in big rooms with bunks. The cubicle was only small but you had a dressing table and a cupboard, a bed with three biscuits[18] and hooks on the door. There were showers where we were billeted at the bottom end of the corridor where our cubicles were. It was very handy – you could get up and have a shower, then get ready to go back on duty. There were no problems with hot water, or rotas or anything – we could just have a shower when we wanted. There was a canteen (it must have been the refectory for the college students), and they catered for people coming off duty at 10 o'clock, with cheese and onion pie, or something like that. The canteen was quite big, with quite a few cooks, but you had to help yourself. The food wasn't bad at all, and there weren't any shortages. If you wanted supper, you had to have a lorry come and pick you up. Sometimes, though, if I'd worked down in a stuffy cellar all night, I used to walk home for a bit of fresh air, and I'd forego my supper, because I felt I didn't need it.

We didn't always get kit inspections there unless we were actually off duty because we had a notice that we could put on our door: 'Do Not Disturb'. We came off night duty at 8.00am, had a bit of breakfast and then we used to go to bed. Sometimes we had to go in again at 5.00pm to 10pm, which wasn't bad. But it got very busy because we did all the transportation, and all the armaments and equipment that were coming from factories and going on trains. We had to type the number that was on the side of [each railway] truck and we knew that it was going down to Dover, for the invasion. We did that for weeks on end; it went on day and night for ages and ages.

We still worked underneath [like in Douglas], but the building was a purpose-built command. We had a rest room there, and if you'd worked so many hours, you had to have half an hour's rest, with a cup of tea. They were well lit [rooms]. The teleprinters were like typewriters, and you typed the message, which you could see, but you had to get onto the teleprinter exchange as well, to send it to wherever you were sending it. You could see what was written because it was on strips of paper, about an inch wide, and it just used to come through the teleprinter. You were supposed to take it off and put it in the bin, but if it was something personal, you didn't. Sometimes they even put us onto the switchboard, but it was very hazardous if you did it in Chester because all the Americans used to butt in. 'How about a date, Honey?' and we weren't allowed to do it, so you had to scrumple it up and put it in your pocket or something, because you sometimes got searched. But they were so free and easy; but we weren't allowed to chat, and they were.

For entertainment in Chester there were two cinemas and quite a few pubs, because it was a tourist place really. There was a girl on our floor who was a fan of Bette Davis, and if there was a Bette Davis film on, she'd go at least three times while it was on in the week, and she used to drag me to it. I didn't go every time! We didn't go very far out of Chester – we weren't supposed to go very far because there was the invasion due. Now there are two Hales in Cheshire, and the Hale that was nearest to home, I could get a train to. You had to tell them where you were going, and I used to say I was going to Hale for the day, then I'd to get the train to Hale and then the bus to home.

There were an awful lot of Americans there. I knew one or two people in Chester, through the army, and through them I met this American, although he was Welsh by birth. He was married with children, and he was an architect, from Atlanta. He was on his own and I think he was a bit lonely. I even took him home to meet my family, because he missed his own family – there was no monkey business going on; we were just friends. He was nice; he took me out to the PX[19] and I got American cigarettes and chocolate, and that. We used to get invited to dances. They had lovely dances and always a decent band. Everything from the Americans was top quality; there was no doubt about it. They treated their troops really well. The only snag was I had to go in uniform, and I was only a private. He was an officer, and some of our girls who were officers were there, and they didn't really like me being there, but they couldn't say anything because I was invited [by my friend], but it was a little bit embarrassing. But the Americans were very free; they didn't stand any nonsense like that from their officers – they were just the same as [the other ranks] in a way.

The only bombs I experienced was when I was at home before I joined up. A landmine exploded in the middle of the road and all our windows went. We had one of our cellars made into a shelter and we used that. It made a huge hole in the road. And Dad said, 'I'm going back to bed'. We had buzz bombs later on – they frightened you to death because you didn't hear them until they got near. They used to be whistling along and they'd drop; there'd be silence and then they'd go bang. I was once staying at the family home of my [future] husband in Manchester and had to stay the night, and I was terrified. Those V1s and V2s were more frightening than any of the other bombs because with those you heard the planes coming over. You didn't hear these missiles.

When we went to the Isle of Man, there were always two gunners on the boat. What good they'd have been I don't know because if any planes came over, I don't think their anti-aircraft guns would've been much use really!

I had a peaceful war. I enjoyed it. I met a nice bunch of girls. People pulled together quite a lot then.

Lance Corporal 296285 Joan Robinson

In 1939, Joan Robinson from Liverpool, decided she wanted to join up, so she and a friend decided to do the deed together.

I was 17 and I had a friend, and we agreed that we'd go into the forces if our parents would sign – your parents had to sign if you were under 18. My friend backed out at the last moment, but I thought, 'I'm going ahead with this'. We'd got so far – we'd had the medicals and everything; so I went in. I was a very shy and protected child of elderly parents, and I'm surprised that they agreed. It was the best thing I ever did – it brought me out of myself, as I was a very quiet child. I used to stammer; but as soon as I got away from home, I didn't stammer at all. Being in the army gave me a lot of confidence.

I went on the train from Liverpool to just outside Aldershot and signed on there. Then they sent me back up, to Edinburgh, so overnight I went on a packed troop train, standing in the corridor,

leaning on the bar of the window in the corridor, trying not to fall asleep. Got there, and they said they wanted people down south: 'You can go and train in Camberley'. So I went, and I didn't sleep that night either – I didn't sleep for two nights and I didn't rest for three days! But I survived and I went to Camberley, to the driving school. There were these very old ambulances, very rickety things

with material doors that they hooked on – very strange. I don't
know where they found them all, but they were what we learnt to
drive in.

That was where I found out that Princess Elizabeth was at this
house in Camberley. It was a beautiful private house, in big gardens.
We were in huts, but she was with the officers in the house. We
didn't know she was there – but then they called us out. 'Will you
come out quickly – Princess Elizabeth's going to change the wheel
of a car!' So, of course, Princess Elizabeth came out of the house.
She was in uniform, and she smiled at us, and acknowledged our
presence while we all stood around. She took the wheel off the
ambulance and put another one on, and we were all applauding her.
She was good and she was very nice. I feel like writing to Prince
Philip and saying, 'Don't worry if your wheels fall off –she can put
them on all right!' She stayed there in Camberley because it was
very quiet round there, and she was quite safe in that house. I
eventually left the driving school because I failed my test, so I went
to Aldershot. We were on a depot where vehicles were built like a
Meccano set[20] and all you could see through the office window was
rows of jeeps and trucks and troop carriers. I was a typist and
sometimes we used to sit and type all night, and then we could sleep
in the daytime. It was pretty hard-going with all the documents they
needed – there were eight copies for one vehicle, and they all had
to be typed with the engine number, and different numbers for
every part of the vehicle which had to be put down. They had to be
put in machines, and that was hard because you had to get the last
copy visible as well. They had to be signed for by the troops who
came into the depot and took the vehicles away, and took them
abroad [by ship], or took them away in planes.

One day I went to the office and there wasn't one vehicle there,
not one! They'd all gone, overnight. The troops had come and taken
them – this was just before the big landing [D-Day]. I just sat there
and thought, 'Where are all the vehicles?' and that was when I
realised that something was going on, because it was all done very
quietly. All night, I believe, there were streams of vehicles going
down south from all the different depots – we were only one of
about 15 depots. And then the planes went over. The sky was full of
aeroplanes; I don't know how they didn't crash they were so close
together. There were thousands of them – you couldn't have put a

pin between them if you'd had a picture. My [future] husband was in one of those planes – he was a paratrooper – but of course I didn't know at the time. He was my boyfriend and he came to see me beforehand. He had hitched from some depot down south. Well, he should never have left because it was a secret [operation] and he could've been court martialled if anybody had found he'd left. He'd skipped the barracks to come and see me in case he got killed. The sergeant said, 'You've got a visitor, Private Robinson. I'll give you two hours, and no more. I'm not supposed to, but I will do.' So we went and sat on the grass in the field next to the office – there was nowhere else we could go and no transport or anything.

Anyway, the next day all the vehicles had gone. We'd sat up all night issuing them, of course, but it hadn't occurred to me there wouldn't be any there in the morning. After the landing, they never came back. We were exhausted but we still had to go back to work – we didn't get time off apart from a couple of hours extra to sleep in.

A lot of things happened in the war, but it's the silly things that stick in your mind. I remember one day we were in the dining room having our dinner. We used to have an officer who would come around and ask if we'd got any complaints, and on this day it was my friend's boyfriend. He came to the table and said, 'Have you any complaints?' and I said, 'Yes. Have a look at this'. I was just on the sponge pudding and I parted it, and there was, baked into it, a chain and a padlock. I said, 'I don't think I can digest this, really, do you?' He took it back to the Mess and then came back with another plate and said, 'The cook says she's very sorry but it was mixed in a hand basin; but it's only kept for mixing puddings in'!

We didn't really have much going on for entertainment. We could go into Aldershot and go to the movies, though, but there were queues there all the time, with the soldiers, so you had to get there early to get in. They might have had something going on in the NAAFI, or they might have had a dance. When that happened, Canadians came and they brought chocolate and sweets, and my God, in the war that was wonderful! All of us who smoked (that was me . . .), swapped cigarettes for chocolate, so that was good. It was only with the foreign troops, not the British ones. They just wanted girls to dance with and to talk to, so we'd stand and talk. I'd ask about their families and where they came from. Sometimes, there were Polish soldiers, but they didn't know how to dance – they didn't have Victor Silvester[21] on the radio like we did. So we had to do old-fashioned waltzes with them. They must have thought we were potty because we couldn't [do it] although in the end we were able to do what they wanted us to. They were very kind, and far from home. If you danced with any of the black soldiers, you got a good telling off from our fellas – they didn't like it at all.

We lived in barracks in Aldershot, where they have the resident troops nowadays, I think. If you had stripes, you had to do Corporal night duty whenever you were on call. You had to check the girls in, and then go round with a torch and see they were in their beds. Sometimes, you'd find two girls in one bed, carrying on. 'And where's your bed then? Right, get in it, then, because I've got to check you're in that bed', so they had to get out and go in their own bed. Some of the girls were a little bit boyish, you know. I was very innocent, so I didn't realise all this then, but looking back, I know now! It was in the instructions what you had to do when you were on duty. You had to check that all the taps were off in the bathrooms, and because there were loads of things to do, I skipped down to make sure the taps were turned off. When I went round, it looked as if they were all off, and everything was all right. Well, there was a very hard frost in the night and then a thaw, and I was sent for to go to Aldershot and see the Sergeant Major right now. 'Did you check that all the taps were turned off?' I told her yes, because nothing had been running. Of course, the thaw in the night: whoosh! The taps were right over the Sergeant Major's bedroom and all the water came down. She kept asking me whether I'd checked the taps, and I said, 'P'raps somebody went into the bathroom after I'd left.' 'Oh.' She hadn't thought of that, you see. She couldn't prove I hadn't done it, and I couldn't prove I had, so we had to leave it as it was. She got a good soaking through her ceiling – to the great pleasure of everybody I told. It certainly happened to the right person!

The barracks was a brick building, with tall windows and they had blinds. There were twelve beds down one side and twelve down the other, and there was a metal shelf over your bed. My case was on there, with all my stuff in a box. It was heated with two big iron stoves with chimneys, a pipe going out, and they were very hot. Sometimes the top of the stove was almost transparent, it was that hot. Well, they had to heat the whole room. We had some nights in, where we had to have our kit cleaned up, folded and put on the pillows; you had to unmake your bed and fold it neat. You had to sew your name on your blanket, and have it all lined up [straight], folded a special way so your name showed. The night officer who was on duty came round to inspect it all. They'd tell us we'd got the best room, but we didn't get any privileges for it. And after they'd gone, we had to make the bed again. We were supposed to be in barracks all night, but as soon as they'd gone, we were out – we used to go to the ATS Club. The WVS[22] used to have a club on in a big hut, and they'd have dance music on. The Canadians were there. We used to go over there and dance; and we'd make our beds when we got back. We had a good social life really.

I must say I enjoyed my time in the army, even thought it was wartime. I had a lot of fun. We were all in the same boat, and we all got on well together; everything was good.

1   The term 'ack-ack' comes from 'AA' (anti-aircraft) in the phonetic alphabet of World War 1, which sounded as 'ack ack' is spoken.

2   For more information about 5.5 calibre guns, see http://en.wikipedia.org/wiki/BL_5.5_inch_Medium_Gun

3   Commonly known as 'doodle bugs' or 'buzz bombs', V1s were missiles fired from Cherbourg. They made a droning noise which then stopped, and they continued to fly for a further 15 seconds before hitting their target. For more information, see http://en.wikipedia.org/wiki/V-1_flying_bomb

4   Phyllis Calvert (1915 – 2002) was a well-known English film, stage and television actress who starred in many films during the 1940s.

5   The Battle of Monte Cassino took place from 17 January to 18 May 1944. For an interesting and reader-friendly assessment of the campaign, see http://www.bbc.co.uk/history/worldwars/wwtwo/battle_cassino_01.shtml

6   Beniamino Gigli (1890 – 1957), an opera singer, was the foremost Italian tenor of his day. For more information, see http://en.wikipedia.org/wiki/Beniamino_Gigli

7   In 1945, US *Liberty Ship Charles Henderson* was anchored in the harbour at Bari, Italy, loaded with 500lb and 1,000lb aircraft bombs and ammunition. On 9 April, it exploded, with the loss of about 300 lives. The explosion is believed to have been an accident rather than the result of enemy action. For a first-hand account see http://liberty-ship.com/html/contributed/hafford(06).html

8   On 29 April 1945 the Germans in Italy signed an instrument of surrender to the effect that hostilities would formally end on 2 May. The signing took place in the Royal Palace, Caserta, which was the HQ of the Allied forces in the Mediterranean.

9   Lyon's Corner Houses existed from 1909 to 1977. Art deco in style, they were situated on or near the corners of Coventry Street, Strand and Tottenham Court Road. Almost like modern day department stores, they also housed several restaurants, each with a different theme and all with their own musicians. These were hugely popular during the war as convenient places to meet, and eat at reasonable prices. For more information, see http://www.kzwp.com/lyons/cornerhouses.htm

10 Portees are lorries that carry guns on their beds. The guns are not fastened down, so they can be quickly offloaded and deployed.

11 *In Town Tonight* was a popular radio programme that ran from 1933 to 1960. For more information, see http://www.whirligig-tv.co.uk/radio/intown.htm

12 A batwoman was a female personal servant to a female officer. A male officer would have a batman.

13 Portsmouth was bombed from July 1940 to May 1944, because of its strategic importance as the home of the Royal Navy. For more information see http://www.welcometoportsmouth.co.uk/the%20blitz.html

14 Wynnstay Hall, near Wrexham, was the seat of the Williams-Wynne family. It is now a hotel.

15 For a more detailed description of an Anderson shelter, see http://en.wikipedia.org/wiki/Air-raid_shelter

16 A teleprinter was an electro-mechanical typewriter. It was used to communicate typed messages from point to point, or point to multipoint over a variety of communications channels. These ranged from a simple electrical connection, such as a pair of wires, to radio and microwave. For more information, see http://en.wikipedia.org/wiki/Teleprinter

17 German and Italian civilians were interned for the duration of the war, in order to prevent any espionage or sabotage.

18 Biscuits were hard mattress pieces, about 2ft/61cm square. The women were issued with three of these and shown how to make them up into a bed by wrapping them in a blanket to avoid them separating during the night.

19 PX was the American equivalent of the NAAFI.

20 Meccano is a model-construction kit comprising reusable metal strips, plates, angle girders, wheels, axles and gears, with nuts and bolts to connect the pieces. It enables the building of working models and mechanical devices. For more information, see http://www.meccano.com/about/index.php

21 Victor Silvester was a musician and band leader whose records sold 75 million copies between the 1930s and the 1980s. For more information, see http://en.wikipedia.org/wiki/Victor_Silvester

22 WVS is the Women's Voluntary Service. For more information see www.historylearningsite.co.uk/womens_voluntary_service.htm

Chapter 2

Women's Auxiliary Air Force—WAAF

The Women's Auxiliary Air Force, or WAAF, was the female branch of the Royal Air Force during the Second World War, and was established in 1939. It had originally started life in April 1918 as the Women's Royal Air Force (WRAF). Its aim had been to provide female mechanics in order to free up men for service, and its ranks swelled as women enrolled in huge numbers. They volunteered for positions as clerks, fitters, drivers, cooks, storekeepers and mechanics. This first WRAF was disbanded in 1920.

During the Second World War, the WAAFs fulfilled many roles including parachute packing, manning barrage balloons, catering, meteorology, radar, transport, telephone and telegraphic duties, although they did not serve as air crew. Like the women in the other services, WAAFs did not go into active combat, but they were as vulnerable to the same dangers as anybody else stationed at military establishments in the UK.

They worked with codes and ciphers, analysed reconnaissance photographs, and performed intelligence operations. WAAFs performed a crucial role in the control and maintenance of aircraft, manning the radar stations and as plotters in the operation rooms, especially during the Battle of Britain.

In 1943, WAAF numbers exceeded 180,000, with over 2,000 women enlisting per week. By the end of the Second World War, however, WAAF enrolment had declined and thousands of women left the service after demobilisation. The remainder, now only several hundred strong, was renamed the Women's Royal Air Force in February 1949.

The Women

Sergeant 2003451 Angela Baddeley

As with many young women at the outbreak of war, Angela Baddeley was pursuing a career that was very different from the one she ended up with, following her decision to join the WAAF.

> In 1939, I was doing a London external degree in company law, and I found it incredibly boring. I met a friend and she had a very smart uniform, and she told me what she was doing. I thought I'd rather do that than be a company secretary, so I dumped the law degree and I joined up at the beginning of the war. My father went beserk at my giving up what would have been a career. I remember him saying to me, 'You're no better than a camp follower', but we were very cosseted and I didn't know what a camp follower was! So I stalked out, and I went.
>
> I went for initial training to, I think, Gloucester; and then I was posted to Sealand just outside Chester, doing just admin work. While I was there, I had a very odd experience. One of the girls, who was from London, had died – I don't know what from and I didn't know her. This girl's body was claimed by the parents and it had to go back to Grays in Essex. As I was the only Londoner there, I was deputed to escort this body from Chester to London. I thought I could just get on a train and go down to London, just like that. Well, it wasn't to be like that! They went into the nearest town and got a dirty great big wreath, and I had to go to stores and get a union flag and a cap, the sort that the girl had been wearing. They drove me into Chester and then said the body was being attached to a guards' van, and it was waiting for me. I got in, and we went on to Crewe, where they said they couldn't take the body any further.
>
> So they took the guards' van off that particular train and we went on to another station, and then on to another place where they said they'd attach us to a Post Office sorting van, which was interesting because you were not allowed to do that sort of thing. The guards' van was attached to the back and I sat on a chair while watching the

men sort [the mail]. Then they said the next train was going from Bedford but [I was] in the wrong part of the railway system because I was where all the goods trains were. So they provided me with a filthy old Pullman coach and attached the guards' van with the coffin on the back and we were shunted until we got to the other side of this marshalling yard. Halfway through all this, a bloke with a lamp came in – it was a bit spooky, as I was in the dark, sitting by myself – and he said, 'I hope you don't mind, Missy, but I've got a sergeant pilot who's being taken somewhere, and he's lost his escort. Do you mind having him as well?' I just said, 'Bring 'em all on – I don't mind!'

We did get to Euston, eventually, and there was an RAF escort for this poor bloke who'd died. But I had to get to Liverpool Street because I was going to Grays in Essex. How do you get from Euston to Liverpool Street with a coffin? You don't go down the escalator! Eventually we got to Liverpool Street and they hitched the guards' van behind the engine, and the passengers were behind that. By this time it was 24 hours since I'd left and I was very tired and probably looking a little dishevelled. I was still carrying this blasted great big wreath and the union flag and what have you.

We eventually got to Grays and on the station were the mother and father weeping. Then, to my horror, a porter had gone to the guards' van with a truck and just plonked the coffin on it and was going to pull it along. So I rushed and put the union flag on it because it looked a bit bare coming off like that. It was all very distressing. The mother and father then realised that I hadn't eaten for 24 hours, so they wanted to take me to Joe Lyons [corner house] but I said I couldn't leave the body, so I put it in the left luggage and got a receipt for it. Poor man must have been horrified, but the funeral people hadn't yet come to collect it. Well, I went home and came back the next day for the funeral. It was most strange but the funeral people told me I was the chief mourner. Well, then we got to the interment and I could see the flag and the cap going down, but I had signed for them, so I went forward and got them before they were interred. Then I went back to Sealand with my flag and cap; and end of incident!

After about a year at Sealand, I decided I wanted to do something more active, so I re-mustered into what was then called radio location but what is now known as radar, and I was one of the original radar operators. I did a course on physics, maths and electricity, and then I was posted as a radar operator [to various] places. I went to a place on the coast, to an experimental unit which was quite interesting. At the beginning of radar, we could only pick up high-flying aircraft, so the [enemy] aircraft could fly underneath the radar. Then the boffins came up with another one which picked up the lower-flying aircraft, but still the enemy could come in on the sea. The navy had ASDIC,[1] which only picked up things under water, but we wanted to see things on the sea, so eventually I got onto this. As part of the experiment, there was a hut the size of a garden shed, and there were two men and me [in the hut], in the dark – you have to be in the dark with radar so you can pick up things [on the screen]. The dipole[2] on top was a round disc, and the whole caboodle went round! Normally you see radar at aircraft stations now and the dipoles go round. Well, these were fixed and the whole thing went round, the shed and everything! But, of course, it was in the dark, so you were unaware that you were going around.

We had a four watch system that consisted of one or two people on the tube, i.e. in the darkness; one person plotting on a map; and another person sending the plots through on the telephone. The 'tube' is CRT – a cathode ray tube; a television tube. The Germans had a special valve that we wanted, so they asked for volunteers to go across with an escort of SAS soldiers and pinch it. Actually, I and several other women volunteered, but they said, 'Don't be so stupid. If you go across and you get caught . . .' It just wasn't possible, so a man went across. I don't know how he did it, but he knew what he was doing. He had a posse of SAS men, and he pinched the valve, called the magnetron valve. I don't know the details because you didn't talk about that sort of thing in wartime. [The chap] didn't even get a medal for that, which makes me very cross, because it was a very brave thing to do. And, of course, that is the valve that's now used in the microwave. It's funny how these wartime things come forward into civilian use.

My last posting was to a place called RAF Kete, in Pembrokeshire, north of Milford Haven. RAF Kete was just a hut on the edge of a cliff! Shifts varied. You'd be on at 8 o'clock in the morning until 12.00pm; or 12.00pm till 4.00pm. The 24 hours of the day were broken up into sections. We didn't get time off, really. Where we were, there wasn't anything to do if you did get time off; we were very isolated at Kete. We were billeted in the nearest village, called Dale, and we had a long walk along the cliff edge to get to the actual ops block. So, when we came off duty, if it was sunny we used to sunbathe on the edge of the cliff. And there was the sea, of course, so we went swimming. It always seemed to be sunny, looking back!

At that time, which was just prior to D-Day, we were plotting and it was very interesting. I was on shipping – people don't realise that it was the air force that plotted the ships; they always think the navy did all this, but it was the RAF. Anyway, we had all these echoes coming along, and plotting down, it was tug-and-tow, tug-and-tow. They were towing down all the Mulberry Harbour bits[3] prior to D-Day. They were all coming down the west coast because they'd been made in [Scotland], and we picked them up on the radar, with the occasional destroyer. I shall always remember D-Day. It was delayed for 24 hours because of the weather, and these tug-and-tows and destroyers came down, and they had to anchor. I shall never forget: the whole of Britain was in a blackout and, looking back, it felt as if we were all waiting. It was very strange. I remember during my shift in the evening I went out on the edge of the cliff, just to see what was happening and to get some fresh air. In the sea, anchored, were these tug-and-tows, but near to shore (there must have been a deep channel there), was a hospital ship. Of course, that was the only one that had any lights on, and it was floodlit; and there was a green band around it and a red cross. You could even hear the men aboard it speaking. It was empty, ready to bring back casualties. And quite silently, after midnight, they set sail. I often wonder how many it brought back, if it was sunk, or whatever.

I shall never forget that air of expectancy, it seemed to me, all over the country; everything in darkness; the atmosphere was tremendous. I often wonder why the Germans didn't suss out that something was happening When D-Day actually came, I did no more than usual; just looking for surface submarines, or U-boats or whatever, and plotting down [the information] for the navy.

After VE Day, I was still plotting the blasted ships so no celebrations! The fishermen used to put to sea, to sneak out and try to do a bit of fishing, but they obviously didn't know where the mines were laid. We had to tell them to get back in quickly or they were going to blow themselves up. But we were all depressed because it had become a routine job. Prior to VE Day, it was exciting because you were looking for the enemy, but come VE Day, you were only looking at your own ships and it wasn't all that interesting! Then the station was closed and, one by one, we were dispersed, and then I was discharged. It was a bit of a damp squib, really.

Section Officer 3327 Edith Heap

Edith Heap initially served in the WAAF as an MT (Motor Transport) driver, but she eventually became a plotter in the operations room, before finally being involved in the briefing and debriefing sessions with the

RAF bombing crews. She saw life in bomber command at the height of the war, experiencing the planning, implementation and aftermath of bombing operations carried out by the Brylcreem Boys.

> On September 4 [1939], I rang mother, and off we went to York to enquire about joining one of the services, and I enquired first at the Army depot. The ATS recruiting officer, a formidable lady, told me imperiously, 'We don't want you – we are full. Try the RAF at Yeadon'. So we set off for the Air Force. I went straight into the office on arrival and reappeared about an hour or so later, having had my medical and signed all the papers for four years to be an MT driver. I was told to go home and await a summons for initial training. So there I was on September 4, a proud member of His Majesty's Forces with no idea what was in store.
>
> A week or so later, I got orders to report to Yeadon with my own pillow, a skirt, flat black laced shoes and changes of underclothes. I could hardly wait, and arrived early. We were told to collect our kit and biscuits, which I thought was kind, expecting a packet [of] and not three square mattresses! We were given a mac, beret and badge, a couple of shirts and collars, a tie, biscuits, blankets and sheets, and sent off to find our huts. They were Lang huts, containing about 30 beds, and we received instruction in the mysteries of making our beds so that the biscuits wouldn't part in the night, and how to stack the bedding for the day. It was freezing cold with ice and snow that October, and the ablutions were across the tarmac at the end of the hangar – cold water only. We were fed and given the rest of the day to settle in, with lights out at 22.15hrs.

A/CW2 (later A/CW1) Heap was an MT driver at first, but in 1940, she became a plotter, stationed at Debden in Essex, and later in Cambridgeshire.

> The ops room was surrounded by earthworks, like a Roman Fort, and the roof was level with the top of the bank, unprotected except by thick reinforced concrete. It was a big room with a balcony for the controller and others who needed a good view. The table was covered with a grid map and had phone points round it, four [at the] top and four [at the] bottom, and it was tilted towards the balcony. We sat round it, just anywhere and put on our headsets and we were initiated into plotting – 'along the passage and up the stairs' was how to find the position to put the arrows. They were in yellow,

red and blue to match the colours on the plotting clock on the wall, divided into five-minute triangles. There was a block of wood for the aircraft's number, height, etc. It was quite simple and we had dummy runs given by the Observer Corps (and offers of dates!). We practised because we needed to be quick and accurate, and we soon mastered the art of keeping an eye on the clock and changing the colours – we'd remove the arrows when the same colour came round again, every 15 minutes, thereby keeping the plot up to date.

The controller selected the positions for each girl in the watch. I was to be RDF1 on the bottom right[4] – that was permanent – and the others were allotted a place too. We could hear all the WT [wireless telegraph] messages to and from the aircraft, so the battles were running commentaries to us, with language none of us had heard before! But we didn't mind because they were anxious occasions and we only cared that our squadrons were OK. There were four watches in all; we were B watch. I can't remember the roster, but it was four hours on/four hours off; with eight hours on, every third night; eight hours off after it; 24 hours off occasionally; 48 hours off once a month; and leave by the watch when due. This meant meals at all hours, before going on and after coming off – baked beans! – and sleep whenever we had time for it.

To us there wasn't any real start to the 'Battle' [of Britain], there were skirmishes and fights over the convoys in the Channel and we lost several pilots. The watches had one or two spare people, to fill in for illness, etc., and during the long night watch we were relieved for 20 minutes in the small hours, because it was hard to concentrate when little was happening. We knitted and wrote letters and chatted. Being RDF1, I was in direct contact with the Command teller and so was the first to know of approaching raids. In fact, I used to say I could hear the Germans taking off in France, because as soon as they were airborne, the radar stations picked them up. Consequently, I had a constant stream of plots being told to me, and the other sector stations, and I kept an almost-subconscious track of raids appearing and disappearing below our sector. The controller would ask in lulls, 'Anything coming up, Edith?' and I told him where any aircraft were and in which direction they were headed.

The controller was always a pilot, either *Hors de Combat* or too old for fighters. Sometimes a raid appeared out of the blue, not having been picked up before the coast, especially when a radar station had been bombed out of action for days at a time. We started to plot as soon as they turned in our direction, and the block was passed along the line as aircraft flew into a new area. We kept an eye on the clock, removing old arrows when due. Blocks carried the raid number, angels (height) and aircraft strength and were put at the head of their respective arrows. So I was busy with no time to worry.

I've been asked if I was frightened under fire. Yes, before and afterwards, but not at the time, and I only remember one girl breaking down. We were shocked, because we'd been brought up not to show our feelings and to keep control. Another girl who sat through our first attack absolutely rigid went home on leave to Ireland and never came back. Calmness reigned amongst the frenzied activity. The controller gave the squadrons the enemy's vectors (speed, direction, height, etc.) and we heard shouts of 'Tally-ho' over the RT [radio], and a running commentary followed. It was grim and tense. We always managed to hear it all, even though we were busy all the time, keeping our eyes on the clock, with fuel states in mind. There were desperate moments when we heard 'Blue Two going down in flames', wondering whether or not he had managed to bale out, and it wasn't always possible to see. Then, 'Who's Blue Two?' because we didn't know which pilot in a flight flew what in a sortie – it changed every time. Then anxious waits for the squadrons to pancake, only to be refuelled and rearmed and up again as quickly as possible. The pilots got so tired that it wasn't unknown for them to fall asleep over the controls on landing, or stagger off to the dispersal hut or deck chair and flake out.

We started to lose pilots all too often – some baled out into the Channel and all places between it and us, and turned up in due course. Some were badly burnt and we learnt how to treat them – look them straight in the eye and behave as though they looked as they had before. Others had stays in hospital with bullet and shrapnel wounds, and returned to battle as soon as possible, after a brief sick leave. In amongst all this, we went out to dinner, the flicks and any party going, though we had to get some sleep and we often slept the clock round in our 24 hrs off. We usually went to bed straight after tea, if going on at midnight, because 4 o'clock in the morning is a dreadful time and we had to be on the ball. We were woken in time to have a meal before going on duty.

We were bombed regularly and one morning when we were going on at 8 o'clock, the siren sounded and we took to our heels as though the hounds of hell were after us, and we shot through the steel door, just before it clanged shut. The raid had sprung from nowhere, and it was a heavy one. Our aircraft were taking off between falling bombs, some tipping into craters and so on, but most got off the deck OK. Furious dog fights followed and then quite suddenly it was all over – the Germans fleeing for France as fast as they could go. When we came out, there were craters everywhere, and an unexploded bomb behind my car. I couldn't move it for days, much to my fury; not till the bomb was dealt with. The casualties were surprisingly small in fact, though there was a direct hit on a shelter killing and wounding some WAAFs and airmen, and an ack ack gunner too, in one of the pits. Everyone got to work to get the station straight again – craters filled in, unexploded bombs marked and so on, and aircraft repaired and serviceable. I must say that the ground crews were fantastic, working round the clock throughout the battle to keep aircraft in the air, and looking after their pilots like fathers.

Once, when we weren't expecting it, the Italian air force launched an attack. Our squadrons shot them down with comparative ease since they were much less experienced than the Germans. The battle took place over the sea, off the Thames estuary and the Italians never repeated a similar attack. Most people were unaware that it ever took place.

Edith became engaged to her boyfriend, Denis, who was one of the pilots. They had recently been busy making their wedding plans, and Edith was expecting her discharge any day. Denis was on a raid one night when Edith was on duty.

On 11 November, 17 Squadron were scrambled in a hurry and, soon in the thick of it, and having had a field day with Stukas the day before, they ploughed in regardless, again. Just before we came off at 1200 hrs, there was a cry of 'Blue Four going down into the drink'. I was paralysed and luckily, because we weren't frantically busy, we were down on the floor for the first and only time, plotting on the blackboard with more time to listen. The battle was over

Section Officer Edith Heap & colleagues in the ops room.

suddenly, as usual, and the aircraft returned to base. One landed very shot up, the pilot dead; and I knew who had gone into the drink, though I could hardly believe it and I allowed myself to hope. They were still not all down when we left ops. I didn't bother with lunch but went up to MT to talk to old friends. When I got back, Bill was waiting for me. They hadn't been able to find me, and hadn't tried the main camp. Denis was missing; no parachute. I was excused going on watch at midnight, so I went to bed, but not to sleep. I couldn't face the controller in the morning. I'm such a water bucket, I was afraid of breaking down if I received any sympathy; so my friend saw him for me, with the request that there should be no telegram, that I would go to tell his parents. I was given leave and cancelled my discharge, which had come through that morning. I set off for London, and gave Ma Wissler [Denis's mother] a ring from a phone box in Dolphin Square, telling her not to be pleased to see me; and I ran upstairs, armed with flowers. I didn't need to say anything: my face was enough. She was wonderful, so brave, and she rang Pop, who came home at once. It's always easier to cope when someone else doesn't, and I'm afraid we had our hands full with him. It still wasn't certain that Denis was dead, though I knew of course, and I think Ma Wissler did too. After a week having heard nothing, one of Denis's other aunts and I went to Martlesham to see if there was any news, though we would have heard if there had been. There was none, and really no hope a ship had picked him up, as so often happened. Air/Sea rescue hadn't found any wreckage, and they were always on the scene quickly. After another few days I returned to Debden.

Denis had indeed been shot down and never came home.

Part of Edith's role was to brief the crews before they went on an operation and then debrief them on their return. Often they'd had a terrifying time during a raid, and would come back in an emotional state.

Group had to be kept informed of all aircraft movements, take off and landing times as they happened and any other incidents pertaining to the op. Sometimes aircraft returned early for one reason or another, and the duty ops debriefed them – just a case of why they had returned, point of turn-round, where the bomb load was jettisoned, and so on. There were anxious moments as the main force returned, waiting for aircraft to come up on RT. Signals kept us up to date and popped in from their office next door as each aircraft called up. Those needing emergency landings took precedence, and we often had crashes on the perimeter. Sometimes aircraft were heard on RT and then vanished – no wreckage ever found.

The crews came in cold and grey, many recovering from terror – we saw them before they got their 'masks' on, some joking and brash with relief. If anyone ever says anything detrimental about crews, let them try it – both bomber and fighter boys were brave beyond belief, flying night after night (and day) to be coned in searchlights, shot at, and attacked by fighters. I've heard it said that crews were drunk or drugged but that's not so. Certainly we drank a lot off duty, but never before ops, and drugs were unknown. As the crews

Section Officer Edith Heap & colleagues debriefing a returned bomber crew.

arrived, we gave them hot coffee, laced with rum if they wanted it, but not all did. They sat down round our tables and told their story, very often an edited edition, particularly after a bad trip – they wanted to get to their bacon and eggs and bed. It was up to us to get it out of them, where the flak was, searchlights and fighter encounters, and where the bomb load was dropped. A photo was automatically taken when the bombs were released and the good ones were brought in for us to plot. Our reports were typed and teleprinted to Group. Meanwhile ground crews worked all out to patch up engines and airframes, so as to be serviceable for air test and ops next day.

Crews were reckoned to be very vulnerable for the first and last five operations. Our loss rates were higher in these categories. I was duty watch keeper when we had a first op crew back early one night. I sat down with the captain and navigator, not needing the rest, but they elected to stay. Automatically we watched crews for signs of twitch, because people would be rested for a period if it became bad. One sergeant, who was very young, caught my eye. I told him he needn't wait but he said he was OK. Then they spun their fairy story – they'd only got half way across the North Sea, and [there was] no apparent reason for return. I told them they could only return if they had engine trouble, illness of a crew member, or other malfunction. The sergeant was beginning to sag, so I asked him if he'd like to lie down while he waited. (We had strategically-placed beds in ops, to rest during the long waits.) Yes he would, so I took him to the ops room and asked my watch keeper if she'd mind him lying on her bed, where she could keep an eye on him, and I left him with her. I was beginning to suspect the real reason for return, though we concocted a story of engine trouble, and where the bombs had been jettisoned – aircraft never landed with a bomb load if it could be avoided, for obvious reasons. The crew were ready to go to their Messes for bacon and eggs, and I went to fetch the young sergeant. My sergeant said he was asleep, but we couldn't rouse him, so we sent for the doctor. When the sick bay boys tried to lift him, he was as stiff as a board, no sag in the middle. The doc said, 'You're looking at someone literally scared stiff', and he was carted off, never to fly again. Obviously the poor boy had gone berserk with terror – he was very young – and they'd been forced to return. The crew were grateful that we kept it quiet and always after that asked me to sit with them for breakfast – we had bacon and eggs too, once debriefing was over. Not often, however, because they were missing a few trips later.

No one I know who had to do with ops ever criticised, or thought badly of, people whose nerve gave. Everyone has their breaking point, and some can stand more than others, as with pain. Some had very bad, rough trips. One pilot used to start weaving half way across the North Sea, and continued until he crossed the coast coming home, making his crew very sick. Some who lacked imagination seemed unconcerned or covered it up well; some jumped at the slightest noise or developed a twitch, or became withdrawn. Others joked, played the fool and played practical jokes with apparent nonchalance.

Some unexplained events took place. We had an aircraft that landed, shot to pieces. It made a perfect landing and pulled up at the end of the runway. The tail gunner emerged but fainted when he was told that the rest of the crew had baled out some time earlier. His intercom had been shot away, so he never heard the order to jump. No one could understand how the aircraft had come into the circuit apparently normally (it was not surprising the RT was silent, quite a frequent occurrence in badly-damaged aircraft), landed and came to a halt without difficulty. My latest crew, short of fuel, did a belly flop straight down an avenue of fruit trees in an orchard, which they couldn't see, tearing off their wings, the crew shaken but unscathed. Actually, it was often the case that if the aircraft was in small pieces, the crew were OK; and if the aircraft looked undamaged, the crew were dead – something to do with impact. One aircraft I was in made a hard landing down the grass, and broke its back, but nobody was injured.

We had a lot of trouble with the Yanks, newly at Bassingbourn with the B17 bombers. Girls weren't allowed to go into Cambridge after dark without male escorts, because there'd been cases of women being dragged off their bicycles, and, at least, attempted rape. There were fights galore between the two services, even involving officers; cars were damaged and blood was everywhere. Our opinion of American performance operationally wasn't high, and they were brash and cocky. They thought nothing of trying to chat you up, even in broad daylight. A private of theirs hove up alongside me one morning with, 'Say, Babe, how about a date?' and got a short answer! You could never get a taxi in London either, because they tipped far more than we did; and you often had a cab pinched when you were halfway through the door. They came into our Messes, at times, having landed in trouble, lost, etc., in full flying kit which definitely wasn't done, and sat down to eat as though they owned the place. Did they imagine they'd have their kit pinched? They talked off the top of their heads about their prowess on ops, to people with far more experience than they had; to say nothing of their appalling and disgusting table manners, and they were generally *personae non grata*.

Then it came to be my turn to take a party of WAAFs to Bassingbourn for an evening out. The Yanks had a dance every few weeks or so. They sent their transport for us and the competition to go was cut throat, much to my disgust. The girls were given cigarettes, flowers, nylons and very often fixed drinks, and they were difficult to round up at the end. Jean, one of the admin girls, said she'd come with me and I was glad of the offer. We had our baths and put on our best blue. Nothing happened and when it got to half past eight, I decided to ring Bassingbourn to see what had happened. I asked the guardroom, 'Has the transport left yet?' 'No, no sign of it', came the answer. 'Well cancel it', I said. 'We can't stand about waiting all evening.' Jean was a bit taken aback by such cavalier treatment, though she didn't want to go any more than I did – it was a thankless task, and the Yanks knew what they could do with their presents as far as we were concerned. I wasn't popular with the girls, but I told them, 'You wouldn't hang around five minutes for our airmen like this, and you're not going to do it for Yanks and their handouts'. My name was mud and when one of the sergeants was truculent, I told her, 'You're newly married and shouldn't be thinking of going anyway'. I knew her and her carryings on and she wasn't going to cheat on her husband if I could stop her!

We had an excellent dance band and each Mess had its own parties. We attended Sergeants' Mess dances by invitation; the same with the airmen's and WAAF Messes. We went to York to dine – Betty's Bar was an infamous place of pick-up for the boys – the flicks and occasionally the theatre, the village pub, and other station parties round about. I think over the years, I've been in every pub in York and Cambridge at one time or another! Sometimes we stayed the night, super to be off camp for once. Often impromptu parties developed in the Mess, and we sang Air Force songs, old and new, and Canadian ones too – specially-adapted tunes to words concocted by those with flair. We knew when to leave the boys to get on with it, without them having to sing 'Goodnight Ladies'! In any case, we hadn't understood the meaning of some of the words in the milder ones. Seems incredible nowadays when you hear the language used by most girls a lot younger than we were!

We were working up to D-Day and were aware that it was imminent and of the build up of forces in the south, but not the point of landing. We were operating day and night on sites on the coast and softening up inland too. We'd had several V1 attacks ourselves – everybody stood and listened when we heard the distinctive throb, waited for the silence with subsequent explosion, and then carried on as though nothing had happened. We never had a direct hit luckily. On the night of 5/6 June, the first crews back reported, 'It's started – the whole Channel is full of ships. There's hardly room to put down a 6d between them'. We were all excited and we waited eagerly for each crew to come in with more details, if apprehensively. It was obvious that Normandy was the invasion point and we could hardly wait to hear more. We operated round the clock until a good foothold was gained, and lost one of our best Aussie crews, shot down on the beach.

Gradually, the army moved inland and we resumed more normal targets. There was an anxious time during the German counter attack, and the Yanks, hopeless as ever, bombed the Canadians in the [Pas de Calais]. Their bombing methods were different from ours. Our crews operated independently, each bombing on his own target time, but Yanks followed their leader and if he made a mistake (frequently), so did all the rest. It wasn't the only time they attacked their allies – they did the same thing, later, at the Battle of the Bulge. Though it's only fair to say that when lines are fluid it's not always easy to know who's where, and recognition signals are not always clear in the heat of battle. Eventually the armies broke out of Normandy and overran the V1 sites quickly. We were attacking Berlin, almost nightly and other targets too; the Yanks by day. It was important to get another port. Mulberry harbour was a long way back stretching supply lines to the limit. We were ordered to breach the sea walls on Walcheren, so that Antwerp could be secured; a great success, but I felt so sorry for the poor Dutch, all their carefully-cultivated land ruined for years to come, to say nothing of their homes.

There was thieving, and though I'd had my silver lipstick stolen by the batwoman, towards the end of the war, it took on greater proportions and they were difficult to catch. Most offenders were posted, the receiving stations duly warned, for without proof nothing could be done and some of them were clever.

Our targets went east with the progress of the army, and it was obviously only a matter of time. Arnhem was a great tragedy and people I'd known all my life were lost. Cassino had been bad enough, though Arnhem was worse – the awful weather being one factor – fog, etc., and the Dutch suffered again. Of course, we were dubious about the part the Yanks played – there'd been rows at command and we had little confidence in their performance when it came to the crunch. Still we pressed on, our targets in Germany being mainly transport centres and railway marshalling yards. The object was to stop the Germans moving troops and equipment to the front. Other targets were related to oil. The Germans were known to be having problems with it so we attacked refineries, etc. I was amused when I was at Rheindahlen in 1968/71. The German clerk, a Silesian, told me he'd been an ack-ack gunner in Romania, and their billets were situated the other side of a wood from their guns. They were nearly always too late to fire at attacking aircraft. By the time the sirens had alerted them, the bombs were dropped and the aircraft gone. Nice to think the enemy could be just as inefficient as ourselves on occasions!

I met some fabulous people, often from humble beginnings, and was let down by others who should have known better. I had a lot of fun and often helpless laughter. Life was light-hearted in spite of tragedy and tears – perhaps because of them. We learnt to handle death and we supported each other through thick and thin. Those six years were the highlight of my life – everybody pulled together and we had lots of fun. And all those handsome young men!

The above extract was adapted from her memoirs with the very kind permission of Section Officer Edith Heap (now Mrs Edith Kup).

Leading Aircraft Woman 2055486 Kathleen Jennings

Kathleen Jennings joined the WAAF in 1942, and became one of the relatively few female flight mechanics and fitters. She'd been working in a clothing factory in Shipley, in Yorkshire, so her life in the WAAF was very different. While her mechanic's job involved a great deal of technical training and quite heavy work, she enjoyed every minute of it. Servicing and maintaining the aircraft was an immensely responsible job since lives literally depended on aeroplanes being in tip-top condition. While the Brylcreem Boys' achievements must never be underrated, neither must the hard work and efficiency of those women who attended to the aircraft in the hangars and on the tarmac. Without them as well, the Battle of Britain may have had a different outcome.

I went on the train to Bridgnorth [Shropshire] and we were kitted out. They just threw things at you if they were ordinary things like so many pairs of knickers which were standard sizes; other things they asked you how big you were. You got a kit bag and you piled everything in, and you had to write your name and number on everything. You had to learn how to polish buttons and your shoes properly, and how to make your bed – the three biscuits and the metal frame. You had a metal bed that folded in two and three biscuits that were straw-filled and the three of them fitted the bed when they were laid out. You had two sheets that were as stiff as a board, and a pillow that was a bolster-shape, just a small one, but I don't think we had any pillow cases – it went under your bottom sheet – and two grey-blue blankets. Every morning you had to fold everything up so it went back into [the original] position, and it had to be tidy. They gave us a mug, and a knife, fork and spoon; but the knife wasn't stainless and the only way you could clean it was when you came out [of the Mess] and there was a big tank of very hot water and you just washed them in that, but there was nothing to dry them on. I couldn't wait to get home and get a stainless one from Mother. I eventually got my own set in the end, that I liked much better. It was quite an eye-opener to go for meals. Nowadays we're used to going into places where you queue up and get your meal, and take it to pay for it. We didn't pay for it, but [getting it] was that principle, which didn't exist in civvie street at all then.

I was only at Bridgnorth for a short time, and then I went to Morecambe for my training, in September 1942. When they were asking me what I wanted to do, they suggested I should be a clerk SD, which is 'special duties', but they didn't say what that was, and I said I didn't want to be a clerk. I told them I wanted to work on aeroplanes, so they signed me up as a flight mechanic. If I had gone as a clerk SD, it would have been with those who did the plotting, and it would've been a very interesting job, but I didn't know that until after the war. At Morecambe, we got inoculated and I got an infection from the inoculation, and ended up in a big hotel which is [now] the Midland Hotel, but then was an RAF hospital. We learnt how to march – we were all in groups with a corporal who had you marching up and down the prom. Then I went to Hednesford [Staffordshire] and I had to go round the camp to book myself in, so everybody knew 'this WAAF is here; she's now part of this camp'. Because we were going to be technical WAAFs, we had to change our uniform. Instead of having two sets of standard uniform, we got battle dress, which was a blouse-type top [bomber jacket style] and trousers, instead of a jacket and skirt, so we felt quite proud of being technical WAAFs.

The training was in the workshops. It's silly when you think about it. I hadn't ever done anything with tools – I don't suppose many of the girls had. Some of them might have done things with bikes or motorbikes, but no ordinary people had cars then, so it was all completely new. They virtually had to say to you, 'This is a screwdriver; this is a hammer; and this is how you use them'! I was there for six months. They had aircraft engines that we were training on. It's funny, it's so familiar to me that I just don't think about it, but later on I worked on the radial engines.[6]

Others would be like the Merlins[7] which went in the Spitfires and Hurricanes, and were V-shaped, like a cylinder on a car. They had four cylinders in line meeting in a V, and the trouble was if you dropped anything, it went down in the middle of this V-shape, so you had to be very careful.

When I finished my training, I was posted to Wymeswold [near Loughborough]. Four if us arrived there, just trained and we were supposed to know what we were doing. We went into this hangar where there were Wellington bombers. The sergeant didn't want us anywhere near his Wellington bombers. They had what they called a trolley ack which was what they used to start the plane engine with, so we were put to servicing these trolley acks. There were Wellingtons out on the tarmac, but I never actually got into one or onto one!

I wasn't there for very long when they decided to send me to Halton in Buckinghamshire. There, I did get to run up a Spitfire and a Hurricane, and sit in them. What they had to do was run the engine, switch off the magneto[8] on one engine and see if it still ran, and then again on the other side, so I did do that. I was an ACW Engine Flight Mechanic, so then I went to train to be a fitter. That was a very involved training, more detailed, really workshop training, with the men and women together.

From there I was sent to Church Lawford, near Rugby, and there I was working in the hangar where they were doing minor and major overhauls. If a plane flew for so many hours, it had to have a

Mrs Kathleen Cove (née Jennings) visits an RAF museum many years after the war and is amused to spot an engine of the type she used to work on.

minor inspection; and after the next stage (I can't remember how many hours), it had to have a major one where you took virtually everything off the plane. You cleaned everything up and made sure it was all alright, and put it all back together again. I was there until D-Day time. From the beginning of that time, there was no leave at all, and everything got on top of me. I got really depressed, so I asked to be moved, and I got moved to Little Rissington, near Cheltenham, and I did the same sort of job there. I liked it there because it was a peacetime station and we were billeted in pre-war airmen's houses, two-bedroom houses. Four of us slept in one bedroom, and we had a happy time there. Three of the girls were electricians so they could get accumulators,[9] so we ended up with a radio, which was very unusual. They could get the accumulators charged up when necessary so we could lie on our beds and listen to the American radio [programmes]. All the songs from that time are very nostalgic; they just take you back and you can see yourself in that room. It was very cold there. I can remember sleeping in my clothes, sometimes even with a beret on to keep my head warm.

Building up to D-Day, all leave was stopped and they started sending people away, especially the men. They were waterproofing engines and vehicles ready for going across, but we didn't know what was going on at the time. Even though I've read now about the sheer numbers of troops down in places like Dorset, in the Midlands I wasn't aware of it at all. But you didn't know things [about the war] like you do now. We never knew anything; occasionally, if there was something really serious, it would come over the Tannoy[10] or it might be put up on daily orders and if you went to look at them, you'd read it. We didn't see newspapers; there'd occasionally be a *Daily Express* in the NAAFI that somebody had left lying around, and there was usually a radio in the NAAFI; otherwise, in many ways you really were isolated from what was happening. But everybody suspected there was a build up to something.

You had to be prepared to fly in any plane that you worked on. There was always the chance that somebody would say, 'Well, come on. You can come on the test flight', but it never happened to me. But we were told in training, 'You've got to work as if you're going to fly in that plane. Make sure you're doing the proper job'. I did fly once from Little Rissington, and I thought that was wonderful. Somebody was going to one of the nearby stations, just a very short journey. We never went very high: I could always see these little fields down below, with the cows in them. I sat on the floor of this aircraft – I don't know whether I had a parachute or not; I can't remember.

I didn't do a shift system, but worked a full day, from 8 o'clock to whenever, until you'd finished the job. Two of the girls in the Nissen hut were on shifts and we were lucky with them because they could always keep the fire in for us, where otherwise you'd come in after the day and find you'd got to light this darn thing. It was a round stove, and we must have had a certain allowance of coal, but it wasn't very much and so you'd sort round to find paper and wood to light it with. At Hednesford, we were in wooden huts and there were two stoves in the middle. My bed was next to [one] so when everybody was freezing, they all sat on the bottom of my bed, either making toast if they'd got some slices of bread, or warming their feet on the stove. The [stoves] were very important things. We didn't get a lot of leave, but we got Saturdays and Sundays off, or perhaps just Saturday afternoon and Sunday. At Hednesford we went to the cinema quite a lot, and sometimes we went to Cannock. Rugeley was another place we went to, and we played table tennis in a centre for service people. When we were at Church Lawford, the Americans were not far away, and there was also a group of black Americans there. The girls who went to the dances got into awful trouble with our men because they danced with these black men, which they thought was terrible. We'd go for a walk, too, because at Hednesford, Cannock Chase was all round and it was very nice. And I read if I had anything to read. But really, your life was inside that camp.

Kathleen went to the University of Nottingham at the age of 60 and her dissertation was on women's experiences during the war.

It was all exciting for me. I was never in any danger – there was nothing like the bombing in London, for example. I enjoyed it all, and I enjoyed writing about it forty years later.

Leading Aircraft Woman 470001 Jenny Parry

Jenny was called up in December 1942, aged 21. At the time, she was working in Bamburgh (Northumberland). She joined the WAAFs and her initial training was at Gloucester. The RAF wanted her to train as a cook because of her background in domestic service. Jenny emphatically refused to do this, however, and opted to be taught to drive, so she was then posted to the RAF training school in Morecambe, where she trained as a Motor Transport Driver and in mechanical maintenance. The training routine was half a day in the garage and half a day on the roads, driving trucks, ambulances, jeeps, 13cwt trucks, and 'aircraft-carriers' which were flatbed lorries.

Jenny's fiancé was a farm-worker and ploughman at Bamburgh, so she applied to be posted to Brunton which was a satellite airfield for Milfield Aerodrome, and was closer to Bamburgh. However, she was sent initially to Milfield for six months in 1943. (She later succeeded in getting her transfer to Brunton.)

At Milfield, Jenny's living accommodation was in a wooden hut, with a dozen beds in a row, a small cubicle for the female corporal, and the ubiquitous iron stove. Toilets and washing facilities were housed in external blocks. Food was provided on the base in the mixed NAAFI canteen and was generous but basic. There were lots of potatoes and vegetables, but meat came only in stews etc.

At the base we got lots of beans on toast, lots of vegetables, a little bit of bacon now and again and stews – but no luxury meats.

You shared duties. You were often on ablutions, cleaning bins and latrines, driving ambulances, driving officers, collecting food and spares. People usually had their own bicycles for getting around the enormous airbase. We took it in our stride because we were young, there was a war on. Looking back now, it's amazing how we just accepted it all.

Jenny told how there was an awful lot of drinking – many of the pilots were drunk every night – as it was the only way they could cope with the extreme stress and the frequent deaths of fellow air crew in training.

There were dances in the NAAFI. We used to go to the Red Lion (though I didn't drink at all in those days). Whenever one of the young pilots was killed in training, they would all smash their glasses in the fireplace. Those pilots were just young lads, you know. A lot of them are still there in Kirknewton churchyard – Australians, Canadians, new Zealanders; 18 and 19 years old.

The Motor Transport section was a large building with trucks, jeeps, aircraft carriers (transporters), and lots of maintenance bays. There was no standing about – if you weren't driving, you were put to work in the garage, cleaning and servicing vehicles. You were made to clean vehicles, change oil and plugs, change tyres – constant maintenance. We didn't need diets or gymnasiums to keep trim [then]!

When she was based at Brunton, Jenny was asked to drive a guard squad out to the remains of a crashed aircraft at Elwick over on the coast near Ross Sands. The crash was just on the roadside directly opposite the farmhouse at Elwick. It was a Hurricane, the pilot was a Canadian. She found it very traumatic to see the pilot's intestines crushed and smeared over the wings of the aircraft.

It was best not to look too closely. You were young and you were tough in those days – you had to be. I don't know what happened to the bodies because we never knew of any funerals – the authorities kept funerals at a distance. That was the only time I ever had to deal with death at Brunton.

Jenny recalled another WAAF friend who went out to a crash site and saw mangled bodies. The girl coped with the actual event at the recovery site, but later collapsed in a dead-faint when she returned to the base.

Jenny was posted to the RAF transport depot at Lords Cricket Ground, London, in 1944, to Number 4 Motor Transport Company. Lords Cricket Ground was the base for all RAF vehicles in London. Her job was to drive RAF officers (including Deputy Air Vice Marshall [Lord] Tedder) to meetings all over London. She also had to drive ambulances and trucks, and to do whatever maintenance was required.

> We also used to do convoy work, which we didn't do at Milfield or Brunton; about 15 or 20 trucks all together, often driving at night through the blackout. We also delivered homing pigeons in large wicker baskets, to various bases.

She once drove a truckload of aluminium 'window' foil (chaff)[11] from London to Kilmarnock with just one other driver. She did it in a fortnight, but she got punished for being 'over her time'. Instead of staying at RAF bases, she had stayed with friends and relatives all the way up the country to save on her expenses!

Once, she was walking in a London street when a V1 flying bomb fell just one row of houses away.

> We were coming up from Lords when this doodlebug came over and we just ran, though you had no idea which way to run when the engine stopped and you knew it was falling to the ground. There were three workmen standing in front of a wooden hut they were building just across the road from me. All three were killed by the blast but the hut was undamaged.

Jenny suffered blast and concussion. Both her eardrums were ruptured and she was left with impaired hearing for the rest of her life.

> The pain and the shock were tremendous. I didn't know what had happened. I felt sick but my body was unharmed, apart from my ruptured eardrums. It was terrifying.

The war ended while Jenny was in London. She experienced both VE Day and V J Day in London, and joined the vast crowds dancing in the streets. She saw the Royal family on the balcony at Buckingham Palace, and was in the crowd waving at the King and Queen.

Jenny returned to Bamburgh and got married in October 1945. There was no fruit available for wedding cakes; no film for wedding photos and no silk or fabric for wedding dresses. However, Eleanor Roosevelt, the wife of the American President, had been instrumental in arranging donations of wedding dresses, so that UK service women could marry in style.

> If you wanted a wedding dress, you saw the WAAF officer and booked one in advance, and they ordered it from a depot. So it arrived, and when I was finished with it, it was sent back and cleaned for the next bride. It was made of [India] linon, which was a very fine [lawn, almost like] silk. It was largely because I was in London that I got [the dress] – if I'd been out in the sticks I may not have known about it.
>
> But we couldn't have any photographs for our wedding because you couldn't get any film. Mostly, people were married in uniform, and often they were married at the last minute – they were on embarkation leave or about to go away. You had to move fast during a war, make your decisions and take your chances.

Jenny saved currants and raisins, begged a handful at a time from the cookhouse at RAF Milfield. Other friends and family saved their dried fruit rations for her.

> When you went home on leave you had to fit in with the rations. I used to get a few raisins and cherries, a little at a time, and I got some icing sugar for the cake.

Jenny (now Mrs Aitchison) was demobbed in December 1945, just two months after her wedding.

Jenny Parry's story has been kindly contributed by Graham White, whose original interview with Jenny formed part of an article he wrote for the May 2009 issue of *The Northumbrian*, available on http://www.the northumbrian.co.uk/109/

Aircraft Woman 458252 Mary Rose

Today we know much about the psychological effects of warfare. Shell shock, scornfully dismissed during the First World War as cowardice (or

neuresthenia, if you were an officer), is recognised today as Post-traumatic Stress Disorder. Keeping morale high during conflict is always a top priority, and there were many ways of trying to achieve this during the Second World War. Rest and relaxation was important, and so too was entertainment. It was no coincidence that people such as Vera Lynn and Gracie Fields were hugely popular, and even today songs such as *We'll Meet Again* and *The White Cliffs of Dover* can make the veterans' eyes fill up.

The Entertainments National Service Association, or ENSA, provided entertainment for the service personnel, with an impressive list of performers including Laurence Olivier and Ralph Richardson. In spite of this, however, ENSA couldn't be everywhere at all times with such highly-regarded performers, so much of the entertainment was substandard. Because of this, the popular translation of the acronym ENSA was 'Every Night Something Awful'.

Where ENSA couldn't provide entertainment, the concert party invariably did. Drawn from among the service personnel themselves, the entertainers of the concert party gave up their free time to both rehearse and perform, without neglecting their primary duties as service men or women. There was a huge pool of talented people, trained in music, drama, dance, etc., and many of these became household names after the war, when they found fame on the radio or in the theatre.

Many others, however, equally talented but not destined for fame and fortune, were to prove crucial in helping to keep up the morale of their fellow fighters. Among them was a driver, Mary Rose, who had been trained in classical singing. Just by chance, she was discovered by her commanding officer, and she went on to give great pleasure to many audiences, as part of the WAAF concert party.

The purpose of the entertainment wasn't always just morale-boosting, however. Fund-raising also came into it, and sometimes for the most surprising causes.

I got my call-up papers on my 21st birthday in September, 1942 and I went to Innsworth near Gloucester and there I was kitted out and so on. Then it was winter and very, very cold. We went to Morecombe to do our training, and we did our square bashing, where we marched up and down the seafront with icicles dropping off our noses, just about; it was desperate.

When I arrived, they asked what I could do. Well, they didn't really give me much choice – they asked, 'Can you drive?' Well, I'd driven since I was 17, so there I was, driving these huge 4-ton trucks. We used to leave at two or three in the morning, and drive up to Lancaster taking blankets and all sorts of things, in case of invasion. When we arrived there, they were waiting for us and the WVS gave us tea and sandwiches. We were qualified drivers so sometimes we took a trainee with us when we drove up, and they drove back while we sat in the back on the tarpaulins.

Then we were all sent off to various camps and I asked if I could be sent to the nearest camp to home, which was Thornaby (near Middlesbrough), so I duly arrived there. Now, Flying Officer Scaith lived in digs near Thornaby, and had his wife staying with him – quite a lot of the flying officers did that – and on Sunday afternoons, he used to take two or three of us home for tea. So it was my turn one weekend, and off I went. We had tea in the dining room and then we moved into the sitting room where there was a beautiful piano, and he said, 'Can any of you play?' I told him I could a bit, though I wasn't very good; but I did play and we had a good old singsong. Well, I didn't tell anybody, but for five years I went to a Professor from the Royal College of Music to study singing, and I'd also sung the solo parts in things like Handel's *Messiah*. Officer Scaith said, 'Good lord, I didn't know you could sing,' and I just told him that's what I'd have loved to have done in the past. And that was the end of that.

Two or three days later, a message came down for me to go down to the drill hall and see Squadron Leader Smith and Flight Lieutenant Somebody-or-other, who both ran this very good concert party called 'Out of the Blue'. They told me they'd heard from Flying Officer Scaith that I could sing, and they produced some dance music. Then I learnt that there were five musicians in the concert party and they'd all been with tiptop bands – Henry Hall, Jack Payne, Joe Loss – and they were jolly good, they were marvellous. There was also a fellow called George Smith (the most handsome, gorgeous fellow you've ever seen!), and he was a tenor who sang with the band, but he didn't particularly like singing dance music, because he'd been with the Carl Rosa [Opera Company]. Well, I told the officers it was no good asking me to sing dance music because I just couldn't, so they gave me a special pass to go home and get my own music. They decided to team up George and myself singing duets, and we sang songs like *I'll See You Again* and *Wunderbar*, things that Nelson Eddy and Jeanette MacDonald[12] used to sing.

Well, the air force was trying to get money towards buying a Spitfire[13] and so they booked various theatres around the region – we went to the Globe at Stockton, Sunderland Empire, Middlesbrough Empire, Middlesbrough Town Hall, and all the theatres in the area, taking a concert called 'Wings for Victory'. In a year we raised a large amount of money. We did it all in our own time and we were jiggered, because we practised and we did our own work – we weren't given any time off to practise – and nobody's work suffered.

Then they decided they wanted to do these concerts in costume, so ENSA sent us the most gorgeous costumes. We went to Hartlepool Empire one Sunday night, and my mother and father came to the concert, and my father said, 'Well, I had no idea – you're like professionals; it was wonderful.' They were absolutely thrilled; my mother was so excited she kept shaking the man next to her and saying, 'That's my daughter up there; that's my daughter!' The man said to her, 'Well, you've got something to be proud of then!'

In 1939, Mary had met Phil, her future husband, and because Mary was at the air force camp and Phil was employed on government work as an accountant, they found it quite a challenge to spend time together. They became engaged and finally, on 20 March 1943, they were married.

Well, then we took a furnished house, and I was still going with the concert party and doing things with them. We were asked to go to Middlesbrough Town Hall where there was going to be a very big concert with the Black Dyke Mills Band.[14] I was a bit miffed because they just handed me the programme and it said, 'Soprano by kind permission of Group Captain Kelly'. Well, they'd never even mentioned it to me beforehand – they could've said 'Would you like to go?'! Anyway, of course, I went, and it was wonderful seeing the Black Dyke Mills Band. One of the things I sang was *The Holy City*. I remember that very well. I had some very nice evening gowns that I kept with me all the time, because, of course, I'd worn them before I went into the air force, and they were still all right.

And then, I found I was having a baby and that was it! So I had to leave the service. They said I could go back afterwards if I wanted, but how could I do that with a new baby?

Life for Mary wasn't all the glamour of the stage and performing – she had her daily duties to perform too! But amid the humdrum of everyday life, there were a few incidents that stick in her memory. Mary remarked how the war was a melting pot and people from all walks of life crossed each other's path ('from titled ladies to pitmen's daughters' – see Corporal Joan Dargie, ATS), and Mary was to discover this for herself.

There was a cinema about a mile down the road and the last bus stopped outside this cinema about midnight, and then people used to just walk up to the camp, and you talked to everybody as you went up. One particular night, I'd been into Richmond to meet Phil, and I was walking up, and I met this very, very nice Pole who spoke very good English – he'd obviously escaped [from Poland]. We were chatting and I said, 'What do you do on the camp, then?' and he said, 'I'm in charge of the pigs'. We did have pigs in some of the [camps] and of course [they ate] all the waste stuff that went through the canteens. I said to him, 'Oh, you look after the pigs. What did you do when you were in Poland?' and he said, 'Actually, I was Count Somebody-or-other'. He spoke beautiful English, and he'd been educated in England. I said, 'Can't they find you anything better than feeding the pigs?' he said, 'I don't mind. I'm safe'. I thought it was such a shame; he was such a lovely man. But, you see, they were lucky to get away, so they didn't mind what [job] they did.

A young man called Charlie Barker was stationed round the corner to me, when we were in the yards with all the vehicles. I knew him because we used to cycle up to the aerodrome together every morning at 7.30 – he lived just round the corner to me, so I'd always meet him – but I couldn't come back with him at night because I'd be practising for the concert party. He'd worked in a furniture shop before the war and now he was [working] where they packed all the parachutes. One day he said, 'Come round and I'll show you how we pack parachutes', which was a very skilled job actually. There was reams and reams of this tangled up silk. 'Ooh,' I said. 'What's this?' It was a faulty parachute, and I thought 'Oh gosh' – I felt the material and it was gorgeous. He asked me, 'Do you want a bit?' and I said, 'Yes'. So I got a lump and I didn't know what to do with it when I got it; but Phil's aunt used to make herself cami-knicks and she made umpteen pairs of cami-knicks with this silk!

Well, by now, Phil was working in Stockton. He told me he didn't want to take sandwiches any more because he was having lunch every day at the WVS – there was a group of men who got together to do this – and Charlie Barker was one of them, because he'd left by then. Well, this went on for years; I'd left [the air force] and we had a house of our own, and Phil was still meeting Charlie for lunch. He had a very small furniture shop by then, and he'd joined up with this Stonehouse man. Well, I had a table that Phil's aunt gave me – a beautiful antique, and I wish I'd kept it, but you know what you're like when you're young: I thought it was old-fashioned. Now, Charlie did take good second-hand furniture, because all you could get then was this utility stuff, and that's how I got my very first dinner-wagon, because I swapped it for this table with Charlie.

He was so nice and ordinary, you'd never have thought he'd end up owning all those posh Barker & Stonehouse shops![15]

Corporal 2071373 Sybil Scudamore

During the war, Bletchley Park[16] of Enigma code fame was the site of Britain's main decryption establishment. Ciphers and codes of several Axis countries were decrypted there, most importantly ciphers generated by the German Enigma and Lorenz machines.

The top secret intelligence produced at Bletchley Park was codenamed Ultra, and is credited with being of vital assistance to the Allied war effort, and with shortening the war. Ultra contributed to the Allied success in defeating the U-boats in the Battle of the Atlantic, and to the British naval victories of the Battle of Cape Matapan and the Battle of North Cape.

While most people will think of the famous cracking of the Enigma code and of Alan Turing when Bletchley is mentioned, it's not well known that women made up the majority of the personnel there, and that they made a significant contribution to the code breaking. Neither, probably, will they know that at the height of the codebreaking endeavours, some 9,000 people were working there.

One of those was Corporal Sybil Scudamore, who was working in Signals. She joined the WAAFs in January 1942 at the age of 24, and was attached to Bletchley Park, in the outstation at Leighton Buzzard. Her task was to take down messages from personnel in the field, who transmitted in Morse code. Through her fingers came news of captured agents, messages from the Allies and other highly sensitive information so crucial to the successful conduct of the war.

I was stationed at Leighton Buzzard which was the next station down the line from Bletchley. I was on special duties as a high-speed wireless telegraph operator. I'd gone from the usual Morse code, [di – dah – dah – dit], to visual where you saw the signal instead. Then you put it through a machine and it went to whatever country you

were working with. It was signals sent by the Allies that we were picking up. We were getting them from Australia and Malta, and all over.

When you came on duty, you'd be doing one of two things. You'd either be receiving and sending, or you'd be writing up the signals on these message pads. You put the message pads onto a belt above you that was moving along all the time, and that went into the cypher queens, the girls who turned the messages to English. The high speed transmission was going at about 120 – 130 words per minute and you were just going non-stop. But there were three levels we worked at: one was 'Stop everything because something very important is coming through'; one was 'Be prepared for something that's coming through'; and then there was just your ordinary work that was coming through.

Sometimes it came through that the agent had been caught by the Germans, which of course, they were. There were English agents who used to hide in the catacombs on some of the little islands around Greece. Arrangements had been made to take a lot of them away from the area on a submarine during the night. The Germans got to know about this and as the agents were swimming out to meet the submarine, or boating for the ones who couldn't swim, they were all shot. I was damn glad, to be honest, that I was a woman during the war; a lot of the men had to do awful things like sticking knives in people and I don't think I could've done it!

We had four shifts on a weekly turnaround: you did 8.00am to 4.00pm; the next week you did 4.00pm to midnight; and in the next shift you did midnight to 8.00am; and then the other week you were on leave.

Lots of the girls were in civilian digs and many of the landladies hated having them. There was one girl whose landlady said to her, 'Pity you couldn't be doing some of the work that I've heard talked about on the radio'. She replied, 'What do you think I'm doing!' and then she went on to tell the woman everything that she was doing. After that, she came rushing down to where I was living and just burst into tears – she was absolutely terrified. I said, 'Come on – let's go and see the police. That's the only thing we can do.' So we went and told them. They said she wasn't to go back there, and they sent somebody to pack her things and bring them away. The policeman went to see the landlady and told her that if she repeated anything that she'd been told, she'd go to prison for at least the rest of the war.

Another time, just before D-Day, they sent about half a dozen soldiers to us, and I was with one of them explaining what he had to do. I told him I would be on duty at midnight, and he said he'd 'be there by then'. Well, I was calling him up all night long but I never got an answer. In the morning, just before going off duty, I heard from him. He sent, in English, the message, 'War, war, war'. It turned out that they'd been in a field where Germans were too, and if he'd answered me, the Germans would have got them.

One or two of Sybil's experiences proved that, contrary to popular belief, not everybody pulled together or helped each other out. The spiv did very well for himself, as we all know, but it wasn't always the spivs who thought of Number One first:

Once, when we were in London, I saw a note on the doorstep, saying, 'Please return the milk – it's for the baby'. Somebody had stolen their milk.

Nor was it always the civilians who were keen to turn a quick quid.

We had the most terrible dinners, the food was awful. I was talking to one of the lorry drivers one day who mentioned he was going to deliver some beef to one of the other WAAF bases. I said I wished we had beef and he said he'd already delivered beef to our place. It turned out they were selling it; they were selling our rations; they were absolutely evil.

And when I joined up, I carefully removed my chocolate ration and my clothes coupons. [The officer} asked me where they were and I just told her I'd used them. Well, she was furious because she was selling them. These were WAAF admin people!

Then, because they gave us the most terrible eating tools, I wrote to my father and asked him to send me a silver knife, fork and spoon, which he did. One girl said, 'Could I borrow your knife, when you're going on leave?' so I said 'Yes', and I never saw it again. That wasn't nice.

Some of the higher ranks, it seems, were happy to throw their weight around, and the services were no different from civvie street in having their share of bullies. Sybil came across one, who was beautiful but an absolute monster, who seemed to have particular pleasure in bullying the sensitive WAAFs.

There was one girl who was like a shaking jelly, afraid of this inspector. I thought if ever one of these girls commits suicide – because we were trained for work, not to be bullied – I thought I won't keep my mouth shut. But nobody ever did, thank goodness. One evening, we were waiting for them to change the settings because of the interference, when suddenly from the other side of the room, this screech came, 'Yooouuuuuu'. My friend said, 'Sybil, she's speaking to you' and I replied, 'My name's Scudamore; I don't answer to "you"'. So she came hurtling over and said, 'What do you think you're doing?' and I said, 'I'm doing the normal thing – I'm waiting for Greg to change the things because of the interference'. Well, she could see she wasn't getting anywhere, so that was that.

In spite of all that, though, I think the war was probably the best time of my life.

1   ASDIC was a system for detecting things under the surface of the sea. For more
    information, see http://jproc.ca/sari/asd_mod.html

2   A dipole antenna was used for transmitting or receiving radio frequency energy. For
    more information, see http://en.wikipedia.org/wiki/Dipole_antenna

3   Mulberry Harbours were temporary harbours used to facilitate the Normandy landings
    in 1944. They were made in sections and assembled just prior to use. For more
    information, see http://en.wikipedia.org/wiki/Mulberry_harbour

4   RDF, or radio direction finder, is a device for finding the direction to a radio source.
    Because of radio's ability to travel very long distances and over the horizon, it makes a
    particularly good navigation system for ships, small boats, and aircraft that might be
    some distance from their destination.

5   For further information on the V1 launch sites, and good colour photographs of the
    site today, see http://coalhousefort-gallery.com/V1-flying-bomb-Vengance-weapon-
    site-Hazebrouck

6   The radial engine is a reciprocating-type internal combustion engine configuration in
    which the cylinders point outward from a central crankshaft like the spokes on a wheel.
    For more information, see http://en.wikipedia.org/wiki/Radial_engine

7   The Rolls-Royce Merlin is a British, liquid-cooled, 27-litre (1,600 cu in) capacity, 60°
    V12 piston aero engine, designed and built by Rolls-Royce Limited. For more
    information, see http://en.wikipedia.org/wiki/Rolls-Royce_Merlin

8   A magneto is an electrical generator that uses permanent magnets to produce pulses of
    high voltage alternating current. For more information, see http://en.wikipedia.org/
    wiki/Magneto_(electrical)

9   An accumulator is an apparatus by means of which energy can be stored, such as a
    rechargeable battery or a hydraulic accumulator.

10 Tannoy is a powered loudspeaker system for studio monitoring and sound
    reinforcement. For more information, see http://www.tannoy.com/

11 Chaff was a radar countermeasure in which aircraft or other targets spread a cloud of
    small, thin pieces of aluminium, metallised glass fibre or plastic, which either appears as
    a cluster of secondary targets on radar screens or swamps the screen with multiple
    returns. For more information, see http://en.wikipedia.
    org/wiki/Chaff_(radar_countermeasure)

12 Nelson Eddy and Jeanette MacDonald were 'America's Singing Sweethearts' of the
    1930s and early 1940s. They made many films together and their duets were very
    popular with the forces during the war. For more information, see
    http://www.nelsoneddy.com/

13 The Spitfire was the famous fighter aircraft that played such a crucial part in the success
    of the Battle of Britain in 1940. For more information, see http://www.spitfiresociety.
    com/

14 The Black Dyke Mills Band (now the Black Dyke Band) is one of the oldest and most famous brass bands in the world. It was started in 1855 in the Black Dyke Mills in Queensbury, Yorkshire, with the members wearing uniforms made from cloth woven in their own mill. For more information, see http://www.blackdyke band.co.uk/

15 Barker & Stonehouse is a well-known chain of upmarket furniture in the UK.

16 Bletchley Park, and its outstations, was the centre for Britain's intelligence operations. Germany believed their Enigma-encrypted communications were impenetrable to the Allies, but the code-breakers at Bletchley cracked the encryptions, and so were able to collect vital intelligence for the remainder of the war. For more information, see http://www.bletchleypark.org.uk

Chapter 3

Women's Royal Naval Service – WRNS

The Women's Royal Naval Service (WRNS) was formed in November 1917, because of heavy naval losses and a shortage of manpower for active sea service. Because the sailors who were shore-based were needed on the ships, women stepped into the breach and carried out their vacated jobs. The slogan to encourage recruitment to the WRNS was 'Join the Wrens – free a man for the fleet'. Over 6,000 women joined, and they fulfilled a variety of duties. The service was operative until it was disbanded in October 1919, but it had made a tremendous impression during its short existence.

When there were the rumblings of war in 1938 – 39, the WRNS was revived. Some 74,000 women, known as Wrens, had joined the service by 1944. They fulfilled duties as cooks, clerks, telegraphers, electricians and a few as air mechanics. Those who joined as nurses were not members of the WRNS, but of the Queen Alexandra's Royal Naval Nursing Service. Many Wrens were also involved in the planning and organisation of naval operations.

The Women

Leading Wren 53330 Margaret Carson

Margaret Carson was working on a dairy farm near Belfast when war broke out. When she applied to join the Wrens, they wouldn't accept her

as she was doing work of national importance. She managed to bypass the regulations, however.

It was 1941 and because they wouldn't take me, I went home and stayed with my mother. I tried again and said I was [living] at home! I was about 20 when I signed up and I went to Mill Hill in London for training. I'd already been to college and got my certificates as a cook, so it was just basic training there, drill, and to get my uniform and so on. I had to sit different [cooking] exams, for all I had my own certificates from home.

Then I was posted to Harwich. We worked all different times; sometimes we used to work until 10 o'clock at night. If I went on early morning, I'd do the breakfasts and stay on until lunchtime; the next shift you'd come on for dinner time. I was preparing all the meals for the ordinary seamen, but sometimes for the officers. It was quite hard work but you were young and you never noticed it. We were billeted in the Cliff Hotel in Doverport, and I worked on the quay, where the Mess was. There were about six other girls billeted with me in the room, in bunk beds. We had a special bus that used to take us down to the docks for whatever time you were going on duty.

Coming up to D-Day, we were cooking more as they were bringing in more people for the invasion. The docks were filled with minesweepers and submarines, and so on, all coming in, and they used to use the Mess a lot, so we had a lot of people coming in. But we didn't know anything about it really because we weren't told. We knew something was going on because our leave had been stopped for quite some time.

I was in the channel for London [air raids] and the doodle bugs were coming over all the time. Some of the hotels were blown up where I was. We had to go in the shelters when the bombing was on. There were benches for you to sit on, and very dull lights. They were underground shelters and purpose-built, made of brick. They were just for us; there were no civilians in there. When the siren went off you hadn't time [for anything] – you'd just pick up what you could and get down. You'd be there for an hour, an hour and a half, until the all-clear would go.

There were Americans galore and we used to get the Liberty boats over to Ipswich and we'd go to the ENSA shows, which the Americans had a lot of, and dances and so on. We had some lovely nights; there were that many good shows, it was cheerful, really. I saw Vera Lynn once. We used to go to the dances a lot; and there was the pictures we used to go to. We had to be back for 10 o'clock unless you were at a dance and you could get a late pass. During the summertime it was lovely because we were out on the beach and we were never out of the sea. There were certain ways you could go, but there were big cement blocks to block it off [against invasion].

We had plenty of food; I couldn't say we had any [shortages] – the food was terrific. Nothing was rationed although you were only allowed so much a portion. You'd have roasts, and fish and chips, and salads, and plenty of fresh vegetables. We had puddings, too: apple tart or apple crumble. There was a victualling store and we'd put in the orders for what we wanted for the menus for the next day, so you were organised. At the weekend, the order would go in for two days. The Wren above me would decide the menus and we'd have to check them over; we met on different days to check the menus together. The menus were on a rota and turned over about once every four weeks.

I was also in a naval hospital in Southend. It was in a big hotel they'd [requisitioned]. The orderlies used to bring the patients their meals from the kitchens. The meals would be put into a special trolley with the [patients'] names on for the different meals. They got a chance to order what they wanted, but there were diets and so on that we had to cook for. The patients were all women and they were in there for ordinary illnesses, not injuries.

I was in London on VE Day – it was only about an hour's run on the train – and I remember everybody went mad. It was very exciting, with the crowds and so on. We went all round, a crowd of us together; it was a very happy time. Nobody was drunk or anything like that, just cheerful; dancing in the streets and music, and all the rest of it. They weren't so strict and so you felt as if you were getting let loose. We went from place to place but then, of course, we had to catch the train back.

It wasn't a sad time for me. I was young and didn't realise the danger. I enjoyed it.

Ordinary Wren Pat Chicken

Pat Chicken was from Workington in Cumbria, and volunteered to join the WRNS in 1944. However, she wasn't called up for duty until three weeks before the war in Europe was officially over, on 8 May, so her military and wartime service were somewhat limited. Nevertheless she was trained and served until she was demobbed in July 1947.

She first went to Headingley in Leeds where she underwent supply training for the fleet air arm. She also saw service in Arbroath, in Scotland, where she was for VE Day, and took part in the celebratory march through the town; and in Winchester. It was while she was a serving Wren that she joined one of the WRNS concert parties.

Performing in the concerts obviously gave her immense pleasure, but it was one particular concert that afforded her a unique experience that she was to remember with pride and affection for the rest of her life.

Her former padre was a cousin of Winston Churchill, and he had become the chaplain to the chapel at Windsor Castle. Through this connection, the concert party was invited in May 1947 to give a performance for the King and Queen, and Princesses Elizabeth and Margaret at Windsor Castle. It was to be the highlight of Pat's time in the Wrens, and the next day, she wrote a nine-page letter home to her parents, giving a fascinating insight into some 'behind the scenes' aspects of royal life.

Monday 19.5.47

Dearest Mother and Dad,

Well, darlings, I think this is going to be the most interesting letter I have ever written, and I have so much to tell you, I hardly think I'll be able to remember everything as it happened.

We were all up very early yesterday, and set off for Windsor in very high spirits. We arrived at Windsor Great Park and had numerous gates opened by men in green uniforms and high hats, and arrived at the tiny chapel in good time for the morning service. We were met by Rev. Churchill (chaplain of the estate, who used to be our padre) who looked splendid in a lovely red robe. He welcomed us in turn and we then went into the chapel. He took us up to the Royal Pew and showed us the King's Bible, a huge book, covered with scarlet velvet and a lovely design worked on it in gold thread and jewels.

Then we sat down and waited for the arrival of the Royal Family. This chapel is not very big, (it is not the one up at the castle! – this one is only a few yards from the Royal Lodge!) but

The members of the naval concert party, including Wren Pat Chicken, which entertained the King, Queen and Princesses Elizabeth & Margaret at Windsor in May 1947.

certainly is the loveliest one I have ever seen. The altar cloth is in a bright, all-coloured weave and looked very homely. The Royal chairs are in light wood and padded with green moquette. The ceiling is pale blue with gold stars all over, and the various plaques around were in marble, ebony, or pale blue and gold. One plaque in particular was a marvellous piece of work. It was the verse – 'I said to the man who stood at the door – give me a light', etc. This was gold lettering on the blue background and the frame was carved in real gold! In a corner, opposite me, was a flag, worked with the Windsor crest and in gold thread was printed – 'To serve – I strive'.

Suddenly a hush came over everyone and the Royal Family were coming in. It was all I could do to stop myself crying, I felt so proud and yet so humble. The King wore plain clothes and looked very old and drawn. Throughout the service, he had his head on his hands as though he felt ill. The Queen sat next to him, dressed in pale lavender with a double row of pearls and a diamond brooch. She still looks very young and very lovely. She kept leaning forward to smile at the people on the estate, as this is their first visit to Windsor, since the Royal Tour.[1] Princess Margaret came next in a lovely pale blue hat with huge flowers on it, and a cream coat and accessories. Elizabeth wore a heavy linen coat of linen in natural shade, pale blue dress, off the face hat, and white shoes, bag and gloves. She kept looking our way when we were kneeling and once she said something to Margaret, and they smiled, then the Queen put her hand out to tell them to keep quiet. During the singing of one hymn, Elizabeth must have thought it was over, because she put down her book and folded her arms! Honestly, I just had to smile!

When the service was over, the Royal Family left first and I hated to see them go. We went out of the ordinary door, and to my amazement and pleasure, I saw them waiting to meet us. We saluted the King, and then formed a line, which they all walked down. The King asked what 'S' meant on one of the boy's arm and pointed to mine and said 'Another one here, I see!' Then the Queen came and I <u>actually shook hands with her</u>. I felt so proud, I thought I would faint! She said 'Good morning' so I replied 'Good morning Madam'. Then she went on to say that we must visit the castle and that it was a pleasure to have us. To which I replied 'It's a great honour to be here, Madam.' The Princesses were not allowed to speak to us, being that their parents were present, but they stood only a few feet away, so we had a very good look at them. Margaret is very pretty indeed, and has the loveliest shade of blue eyes I have ever seen. They have both gone slimmer since they went to S. Africa. They all said 'Goodbye', and walked over to the Lodge. Elizabeth was last, and suddenly she saw her corgi dog and ran to it with arms outstretched. It was just as any girl would have done!

Well, all the excitement over, we went into the bus and went to the Chaplain's house for lunch. Then trooped into the bus again and went up to the castle. It was closed to the public, as the Royal Family are staying there in June, and so we were the only people allowed in. Gosh, it was a sight worth seeing! The first room we saw was full of crockery of every shape and size and the designs were really lovely. The guide floodlit the cases and they looked even better then. I asked him if it was ever used and he said 'Yes – whenever there was a banquet'. Then we went up the Grand Staircase and were confronted by dozens of suits of armour, swords, guns and all kinds of flags. One suit of armour belonged to Henry VIII and it looked just like him! We carried on through the seventeen state rooms we were allowed to visit and everywhere we were amazed at the splendour of everything! There were two solid silver tables, all carved out, and it takes four men to lift one of them! The carpet in the Banqueting Hall is 80ft by 40ft [24.3m by 12.1m]. The only one in the world in one piece as large as that! It was made by convicts in India, and took seven years to do. It weighs two tons, so you can guess what it looked like! The table in this Hall was 'compressed' down to about 50ft [15.24m] and when fully opened out, can seat 150 people with ease.

The oil paintings on the walls were absolutely priceless! All by old masters, and the ladies on some of them were really beautiful. The things that appealed to me, though, were the Tapestries! We think ours is lovely at home! Crikey, you want to see these! There's every colour imaginable in them and the size is terrific! Some of the ceilings are painted with ornate decorations of banquets and so forth. They were done as far back as the 15th and 16th centuries, and took years to do. Then the chandeliers were lit, and the result must be seen to be believed! Thousands of points of colour, flashing all over the place and making the room look like a mine of colours. It was all so breathtaking I feel that you are not getting my descriptions as ever as I can see them in my mind's eye!

There were swords with hilts of every precious stone imaginable. Crowns from various countries and a big gold peacock studded with all coloured stones, which was a masterpiece of work! They must be worth millions, all these things you know! In one room there were two skins of Bengal

King George VI at Windsor when Wren Pat Chicken was in the concert given for the royal family.

tigers – 8½ ft long! [2.59m] Honestly, there were so many different things to see, I just can't bring them all to mind!

We eventually came to the last room and from there, we went to St George's Chapel and saw all the tombs of various kings. Beside the statue of George V there is a space for the Queen Mother! Afterwards, we rode around the Park and climbed up a big hill to a statue of George III mounted on a horse. From there, there runs a straight road right up to the castle – 3 miles [4.8Km] away and it was a sight to see! We all stood for a photograph here, but as it drizzled all day, we don't know whether they will come out! After this, we carried on to the gardens, and here again, we were amazed at the variety of colours of azaleas and shrubs. The sunken lakes were full of lilies, but of course the flowers aren't out yet! There were two trees there from India, and the bark on them was red and highly polished. I should think they would make lovely furniture!

Princess Margaret at Windsor on the day of Wren Pat Chicken's concert.

By this time, we were awfully hungry, so we made our way to 'Big Eats'. We all tucked in and it wasn't long before the plates were empty and we were all really full!

Well, it was getting on for 7.30 now, so we started to get ready for the show. Gosh, how everyone enjoyed it! They didn't want it to end at all. Afterwards, we danced in the hall for about an hour and set off for home about ten thirty. I was absolutely dead beat, and fell sound asleep on a [?]'s shoulder. It was midnight when we got back and after a hot cup of coffee, I tumbled into bed and slept like a log until it was Rising Bell. Now, here I am, still tired, but thinking of it all, and remembering it as the most marvellous outing in my life!

It was all most impressive, but I just said to one of the boys – Give me my own home, for all this!

Well, dears, that is all for the present. My fingers are aching with writing so much, but I knew you would be waiting to hear how I enjoyed myself.

Hoping you are both well.
Dearest love from
Pat

PS We even went into the private chapel in the state rooms, where all Royalty are christened and confirmed. It is semi-rectangular and very lovely. The public aren't allowed there as a rule! – the King gave us special permission! We have also left our programmes to be autographed!

Wren Chicken was demobbed on 15 July 1947, went home on 16 July and met her future husband on 17 July – clearly a very busy few days! Wren Pat Chicken's letter has been reproduced by kind permission of her daughter, Mrs Judith Bryson.

Leading Wren 9374 Doris Hatcher

Working in Blyth, Northumberland on the day war broke out, Doris Hatcher was told to go home, which she did, and she didn't return to that job at all. In 1940, she applied to join the WRNS.

I was called up to go to the barracks in Blyth, and I was seventeen and a half years old. There was what was called mobile and

immobile (you couldn't move away). As I was living in Blyth, which was a naval port, I had to stay in Blyth. I lived at home and I got a boarding allowance; that was immobile. There were only three things you could do: cleaner, cook or messenger. I said I'd be a messenger. There was one other girl and me. There was an office with telegraphers, taking the signals, and teleprinters and coders, and switchboard operators. This was in a building on the docks. Along the walls there were cubicles with slots for signals to go in. The signals came in, were decoded and typed up onto a signals form, then put into these pigeonholes, for the ships that were in, or for the submarines. There were also signals that had to go to the offices inside the building. We used to go down to the harbour on our bikes and take our signals to the ships. The signals were about things of the day; what had to be done; instructions from the Admiralty, and so on.

When we came back, we had to work. There was the Chief Yeoman who taught us how to do everything. He taught us how to do the signals as they came in, how to be a teleprinter, a decoder or a switchboard operator. There were four watches from 8.00am to 12.30; from 12.30 to 6.00pm; from 6.00pm to 12.00am; and from12.00 to 8.00 the next morning. Then they had 24 hours off. I got a job as a switchboard operator and I stayed there for three years. Then they asked me if I would go mobile and go up to Scotland, so in 1943, I went to Inverness. It was terrible. The telephone exchange wasn't finished and there was nowhere for us to work. We lived in the Cameron Highlanders' barracks and there were 50 in a room, and we were in bunks. We lived in huts and we had no heating, just a stove at the bottom of the room and one at the side. They couldn't be lit until 4 o'clock in the afternoon, so if you were off duty, you wouldn't want to stay in there; and if you were sleeping in bed after a night watch, you were cold! We had no baths and no toilet (but that only lasted a little while until they put the toilets in); the washbasins were in a row of eight and we all had to wash ourselves that way. When we were off duty, we used to go to Inverness, to the public baths, and then to the WVS, to have a bath. Then they fixed up our showers and baths in a shed round the corner, so that was a bit nearer. We were watch-keepers and we worked shifts; there were eight of us on the switchboard, and we were working with the army.

When we were off duty we used to go to Inverness to the cinema or to the NAAFI. We used to have a big notice board in the dining room and we'd put our names down to go to a dance. Trucks used to come from different army camps and pick us up – 'passion trucks', they were called – and take us to a dance, miles out; we'd go for the food really! We'd have a dance, and supper, then they'd fetch us back, and we'd be back at 12 o'clock. We had to be back by 10 o'clock unless you had a late pass, when you could be out until 11 o'clock – the dance would finish at 11, but by the time you got back it would be 12 o'clock, and if it was a long way out, we'd come home earlier. When I was at Blyth, we had tickets for Vera Lynn in Newcastle. She invited some of us to the back of the stage, and we went in to see her; we talked to her and I had her autograph.

Then in March, 1944, I was sent south to the holding base in Southsea, near Portsmouth. I was doing the same job there, but I was dealing mostly with Americans, in tug control. These tugs were very big boats and they were all to do with the Mulberry harbours. When we looked out of the tower where we worked, we could see all the ships for the ready. Around the time of the D-Day landings, it was very intense work. There were all our soldiers and tanks, making their way down into Portsmouth and Gosport to go on board. Out in the Solent was a liner and we used to be in touch with it all the time by telephone, and there used to be soldiers on it. One day, when I went on duty, the ships were all there; when I came back the next day, they'd all gone and just the liner was there.

When I'd been in the sick bay for four days, I saw this long room with all these beds in it, made up, on both sides of the room. I wondered what they were all for and a nurse came along. She said, 'You know what they're for, don't you?' I looked at her and then the penny dropped. That's when all the business hit me most, when I saw the beds, all these lovely white beds made up and waiting.

Ordinary Wren 46632 Mary Hunter

When war broke out, Mary Hunter was still at school in Newcastle upon Tyne, and she was 16 years old. She and her friends nearly all volunteered for the WRNS as soon as they could; but when she left school, she went to work in Corbridge, Northumberland at the Petroleum Board. When she finally joined the WRNS, she became one of those women who spent the war working with guns and ammunition.

> I put my name down but I had to wait until I was old enough, but it was actually longer because, by the time you got an interview and medical, it was quite a while. I was called up in 1942 and I went to Mill Hill in London, for a month's probation. That was horrible for us because we had to scrub floors and corridors and stairs; you'd no sooner got them done than people walked on them, so you started again. But I think it was all part of [discovering] if you were going to be suitable. We didn't get about very much. You were more or less

locked in doing all the [training]. I can't remember going anywhere much in the evenings, but there was always something going on in the place, sort of entertainment.

Then you were given the categories and I chose qualified ordnance because I hadn't much experience of anything else really. Qualified ordnance covered everything in small arms: pistols, rifles and Orlicans [see below]. I tried to get something a bit different, so gunnery it was, and that was it. I went to Whale Island, to the gunnery school, *HMS Excellent* in Portsmouth and we did a month's training there. That was a very strict place and the gunner's mate took you for drill and all that sort of stuff, as well as trained you to undo all the guns, clean them and put them together again. You also had to do a bit of writing about it. We worked with hand pistols that the officers had on the ships and rifles for the men, and there were Orlicans which were on gun mountings. The Orlican was a biggish gun mounted on the craft, but the rifles were just hanging in slots along the ship's Mess deck. The officers' guns were put in cabinets. We had to clean the guns with rags and oil.

We had to pass a test at the end, to see if we could do it, I suppose. The training was all day, more or less ordinary working hours. We were billeted in Portsmouth in a new block of flats which were horrible because they were still damp from just being built. We had to fire watch if there was an air raid, and, of course, there were always air raids in Portsmouth because of all the big ships coming in and going out. You had to go on the roof as the bombs were coming down, watching for fires. It never dawned on us that we might have been killed. I haven't thought about that until now! I remember coming back from leave and getting out at Portsmouth station and I couldn't recognise it – it was all flattened. There was a nice YMCA and it was gone, with all the rubble just there.

I was in Portsmouth for a month and then I went to the Firth of Forth in Scotland, where the flotillas of landing craft came in. We were billeted in a big house called Tidings Hill and there were four of us sharing the cabin [bedroom], in bunks. They had blue and white counterpanes with an anchor on. There was a Mess in the house where we had all our meals. The food was alright; I didn't mind it. It was nothing special, baked beans, herrings and tomato sauce (although I didn't much care for that), corned beef and that sort of stuff, but it was alright; it wasn't bad, really.

I was [working] on landing craft all the time. When a flotilla came in, it would fill the dockyard, because it was a small place and there were quite a lot of them. We'd do the guns, clean them because they'd been on gunnery trials and so on. Then we'd go for the ammunition from an arsenal which was over on the other side of the river. We'd go with one of the Wren drivers. I was thinking the other day she wasn't a very good driver, and there we were with all this ammunition in the lorry; I wouldn't like to go with her now!

We'd bring the ammunition back and then we'd get the boat ready for sailing; after that, they'd just disappear and another lot would come in. One or two American landing craft came in but it wasn't a regular thing. That was alright but they were never as good as ours, although you used to get American cigarettes – they seemed to have a lot more stuff than we had. A lot of landing craft came in but we were mainly on landing craft tanks, LCTs.[2] Again the hours were like a working day.

In the evenings we went to dances and parties. We went on board some of the ships and had a party or drinks. We had ENSA and stuff like that. Once there was Ann Sheridan.[3] They had a lot of shows at the camps and we used to go to them. There was singing and dancing, telling jokes and sketches. We used to go to a lot of dances, of course. It was lovely; we had a good time. It's an awful thing to say, but we had quite a lot of fun and made a lot of friends.

It was sad when you heard of the landing craft going over on D-Day, and all the boys that you knew who were just 18 or 19 years old, were lost. That was sad. We'd helped to prepare the craft, and then they just disappeared. We never knew when they were going. We had some idea they were ready; there were rumours, you know: 'We'll be going soon'. In the build-up to D-Day it got busier, of course. There were more craft coming in and more to do. Leave was partly stopped at least six months before.

I was in Portsmouth on VE Day and it was hilarious. All the sailors were drunk, having a good time, just celebrating, as you can imagine. We went along with them and had a good time; we stayed out just about all night! Before that, though, we had to be in at a certain time at night.

Then I went to Hayling Island and it was nice there because the war was nearly over. We used to go to the RAF dances on Thorney Island. There were always plenty of partners. We did a bit of gunnery trials with some marines but the pressure was all off once D-Day was over. We took the craft out and fired the guns. I didn't do that myself but we were on the boats that did it while the marines were training. We were quite pleased because the marines were seasick and we weren't! Then I went to Northney [Hayling Island][3] and the war finished. It was nice there. We sat on the beach at night and watched the *Queen Elizabeth* and the other ships come back all dressed in their flags. It was lovely.

We were never frightened. We never thought about it, really; but when you're young, you don't, do you? If you can say you could have a good war, well, we really did have a good war!

Leading Wren 51064 Edith Keating

Edith Keating was working in an office in Newcastle upon Tyne when war broke out. She volunteered for the WRNS in 1942 and, having had her interview and medical, she received her call-up papers on 1 January 1943, to report to Mill Hill, London, on 13 January. She was 19 years old.

I remember it was a snowy morning and, of course, all the stations were in darkness. I had to find my way to Mill Hill which was a centre for all the arriving Wrens, and I was there for three or four weeks. I had to don navy overalls and scrub floors, and by the time you'd cleaned one flight of stairs, you were told, 'Right, now change the water and do it all over again'. This was to make you accept the discipline. It was a voluntary service – you could still walk out if you wanted to, but once I'd committed myself, that was it. Most of the nights there, we had to take our blankets and pillows and go down to the cellars for air raid drill.

Then I was sent to Stanmore, in Middlesex, and I had a couple of interviews. I was asked if I would join this category, but they couldn't tell me very much about it. It was secret work and I couldn't tell anybody what I was going to do. I was going to be classed as a Confidential Writer and once I was committed, that was it. I had a few days to think about it, and I said I would do it. Then we were taken to the ex-Spirella corset company factory [Letchworth], where the people were making the drums that went on the coding machines. We still didn't know very much about it, but we were told that we'd be working these big machines which would decode German messages. I signed the Official Secrets Act – you got two years in prison if you spoke about your work; you couldn't keep a diary; you hadn't to discuss your work at all, even when home on leave.

I was transferred to Bletchley Park. You had these huge machines called Bombes[4], and you had to plug in the back of the machine. The training took several weeks, with intermittent exams as the running of the Bombes was quite intricate. They were bronze-coloured cabinets, about eight feet [2.43m] high and seven feet

[2.13m] wide. The front housed rows of multicoloured circular drums and inside each drum was a multitude of wires. We had to adjust each wire very carefully with tweezers. Every drum had the alphabet on, and if two wires at the back [touched], you could have missed a stop, so we had to use tweezers to make sure the little wires were completely straight and the electric circuits didn't short. The back of the machine was a mass of dangling plugs on rows of letters and numbers, and each plug was a thick plait of wire. Apparently there were eight miles [12.8km] of this tiny, little red wiring in the machines. We were given what was called a menu, which we used to put on a peg, and which was a complicated drawing of numbers and sets of letters from which we plugged up the back of the machine, and then the drums would 'connect'.

It was quite heavy work and it had to be done at top speed – accuracy was essential. The Bombes would suddenly stop, and we took readings which were put onto checking machines. If the letters appeared to be matching the menu, the Enigma[5] wheel setting had been found for that particular code.

To make things more difficult, the Germans changed the setting every 24 hours. The readings were phoned through to another part of Bletchley Park and the complete message was decoded and translated. We had a teleprinter at the side of the Bombe and every now and again the letters would be printed out, and we would take this to a little hatch in the hut. It would be recorded and sent over to another hut, and they would take it further on. But the letters meant nothing to us. Sometimes, we were told 'the job came up', which meant that a particular set of letters was beneficial to

The Bombe machine used at Bletchley for captured German signals.

whichever hut it was sent to, and the code had been broken. You felt good. But there again you could go on for days and nothing happened.

Each hut worked separately and we didn't know what other huts were doing, and we didn't ever go into any other hut. The watches were of four-week duration: 8.00am – 4.00pm, for seven days; 4.00pm – midnight for another seven days; midnight – 8.00am for the next seven days; a hectic three days of eight hours on, eight hours off; and at the end of that we got four days off. We mainly just wanted to sleep because your sleep patterns were completely haywire. There were 14 Wrens on our watch, with some RAF men who serviced the machines and they were called I/C Ops [in charge of operations].

I lived at Crawley Grange which was about 13 miles from Bletchley, and it was a big Tudor manor which was built for Cardinal Wolsey, and Elizabeth I had stayed there. It was a beautiful place but very isolated. It was very cold and dark, covered with creeper, and always short of water in summer. There were 14 of us in the cabin [bedroom], in double bunks, and we were all on the same watch, so there wasn't disturbance when we were trying to sleep. If you did want to go out, or be off early, you'd sneak your clothes into the bathroom and get dressed there. All you did was go back from watch and go to bed – there wasn't much of a social life really, because it was remote. We could walk three miles to the crossroads and pick up RAF transport to take us to their dances, or the cinema. They'd collect us in a lorry and take us to their camp. Sometimes we were picked up in lorries by Americans and we went to their dances mainly for the food because it was wonderful!

I've no regrets about joining. I made lifelong friendships and I thoroughly enjoyed all of it.

Leading Wren 48444 Janet Murray

Janet Murray joined the WRNS in 1943, when she was 18 years old. She lived in Crosby, near Liverpool, and by a lucky chance she was posted to Liverpool, as a pay writer. She was there through most of the shocking blitz that Liverpool went through, because of its strategic importance as a port.

The WRNS was entirely made up of volunteers – there were no conscripts; they were all volunteers. Unique to them again, was a two-week probationary period. If you'd passed your medical and before you were officially enrolled, you went to a holding depot. You wore your own clothes, you just had a band round, and, at the end of those two weeks, you could say you didn't want to be in; or they could say they didn't want you. At this holding depot there was every type of person, from the low to the high; it was a good cross section. We were once being inspected by the then Duchess of Kent, who was Princess Marina, and I was standing next to a girl. All I can remember about her was that her first name was Phoebe and when the Duchess of Kent came to us, she stopped and said, 'Hello, Phoebe. How are you?' and it turned out that this one next to me was really high up. I'm glad I went because it made me get down to earth. My mother had spoiled me, I think, and it made me look out for myself. It was pure chance I got to Liverpool – I'd lived in Crosby, but then I was in quarters outside Liverpool.

I was a pay writer. If a ship came in, the sailors immediately wanted their pay, because they'd been away, and [they had] no money, and we'd have to be there to work it all out. In the office in the Liver Building, there were about 150 or so workers. It was called BAO, Base Accounts Office. On most of the desks was a man who'd done his sea time but they were still in the navy; older men who were Chief Petty Officers, that type of people; and they had Wrens helping them. They didn't want us at first. They said we were just school kids; but I suppose, to them, we were, even though we thought we were grown up. They weren't nice – they'd swear at you but you just took no notice. When I first went, I had four destroyers to look after. One of them was the *Starling*, which was a very famous one which caught the most submarines.[6] When the captain died, he had a state funeral in Liverpool, he was so famous. He was a hero really. We had to march behind.

We worked from half-past eight in the morning, to half-past six, with only about three quarters of an hour for a break. One week we had Saturday afternoon and Sunday off, but the next week we only had Sunday afternoon off, and occasionally you had to do a night shift. We worked under such intense lighting that many had eye trouble or fainted. We had big ledgers; no adding machines; no computers, of course; and we just had to sit and add columns. I got picked for that because I did well in maths, and immediately I was told what I was to do. Not a lot of the girls were interested in doing

that sort of work; they were interested in the more glamorous things. The work was quite intense and if it didn't add up, you had all these columns to go through again. They used to come round in the mornings with a big box with what work was yours. The sailors still got their rum every day but for anyone under 18, we used to put 'UA' [next to their name] for 'under age' because they couldn't have grog, they couldn't have their rum. So when you were working out their pay, they got 4d or whatever it was, in lieu of the rum. If someone didn't take it [by choice], there would be a mark on the ledger, and they got the 4d, but most of them took it; in fact, I don't think I came across anyone who didn't have it. There were always people getting transferred or they'd [died]. One of my ships got sunk so I had to write 'D' for 'death' on [the names in the ledgers]. That happened all the time, with ships being sunk all over the place, so that wasn't a nice job.

Occasionally we went to the pictures, but we had no money, you know. Often my parents subbed me, which they shouldn't have done, but [the pay] was only £1.18s a fortnight. We found a little place in Liverpool, run by a Christian society who served us beans on toast for 4d so things were relative, I suppose, but we didn't have a lot of money. A lot of times we just had to stay in, or we just went for a walk or something, but the raids were on, so mostly we were down in the cellars. The Americans took over the Birkdale Palace Hotel and Lord Derby's place at Sefton. We were invited there, and they even had Lord Derby's butler, so when we went in, we used to see this butler there. We'd go for dances and I remember the floor was covered in sugar because it was falling off the doughnuts there was so much of it. They had everything – they must've brought all the food from America. I used to think, 'These ships should be carrying vital supplies', but they were carrying every luxury under the sun! It could be hairy when you went there because they were always after other things, if you get what I mean. When the ships came into dock for cleaning, or whatever, the crew had to leave, but they always had a skeleton crew left, and the officers used to invite us for a meal. That was nice because we got waited on. We'd really go for the food, but sometimes, again, it was hairy! We were taken over some of the ships and we realised how confined they were, and it was all grey. They were all painted with camouflage so everything was dark and dull. Once there was a U-boat. They'd captured it and it was in Liverpool, and we were taken over that. It was claustrophobic with very little room – I'd have hated to be in a submarine. I think they took it up the Manchester Ship Canal, on the surface, for exhibition; it was a sort of morale booster that they'd caught this U-boat intact.

I was still at school when war broke out, and at first it was all quiet. But then we had quite a lot of bombs around us. My stepfather had under the stairs reinforced and we used to go under that. There was a big communal air raid shelter nearby but my stepfather wouldn't go in it. A landmine was dropped and everyone in the shelter was killed; not a mark on them, the air had been sucked out of their lungs. We had our windows blown out and I remember we had a little radio and that was blown across the [room] but we weren't hurt at all. Leslie [Janet's future husband] had just started work then in Liverpool and he had to go on fire watch. He was up on the roof when the whole place went ablaze, and he said that in some ways it was scarier than the raids. He was only 17. It was quite hairy in the raids. Leslie and I had been to the pictures and we were walking along and a raid started and we started dashing home, and we came across a head. It upset me, of course, but we just got hardened to it. You just took things day by day.

When I was in the Wrens, working in the Liver Building, sometimes we got caught in raids. We had shelters which were down in the cellars and they'd been reinforced, so we used to go there. Mostly the raids were at night, though, so we were in our quarters; we had very few day raids in Liverpool when I was there. We used to just go down in the shelter and if we were out, we'd have to try and find the nearest one. All over the place there were public ones which had been built. The station was used for shelter, like they were in London, although it wasn't underground. All along the pavements there were pipes for the water. It was the blackout and you weren't allowed a torch or anything, and I had a couple of falls tripping over these blinking pipes going all along the gutters.

Our quarters were in big houses they'd commandeered just outside Liverpool, and there were four of us in a cabin, in steel bunks which were not very comfy. There was a communal kitchen and the stewards stationed there cleaned. We were allowed three baths a week, on a rota. Ours was in a sort of shed in the garden; it was a long room with about eight baths all in a row. The baths had a big blue line going round and you couldn't have water above it, you could only have five inches of water − I love my baths now! The worst part was that you had to do your own laundering, so there was a laundry room with an iron. We had a clean blouse every day; our collars were stiff and they had to go to the Chinese laundry.

When Leslie was training in Canada, he sent me three pairs of black nylons. They were gorgeous, and I was the envy of the whole place. They were sheer, with just this black line on. I wore them constantly, and they never laddered and never clicked. Someone said afterwards they stopped making them because there were no sales − they lasted so long. If you were on parade, you had to wear the thick [stockings] which you kept in your drawer, because you never wore them otherwise. And you didn't wear the knickers, which we called 'blackout'. They were pure silk but they were these old fashioned ones, and you only put them on if you were on parade, because you got inspected; or if you went on board a ship because the fellas used to make you climb up first, to have a good look!

When I was at the Liver Building, we had to do squad drill three or four times a week, and we did that on the roof. It was freezing and windy but we had to do it. We were marching up and down and saluting, and all this sort of thing. There was a little chapel in the Liver Building and we went to communion once a week; we were allowed half an hour off for that, but otherwise you were at your desk. There was what they called a tea trolley and a sailor that only had one arm used to bring round a beaker of tea at about 10 o'clock, but you had to have it at your desk. The only time you were allowed to get up was if you had to go to the loo. It was quite strict, and if you were late, which made work for anyone doing the pay, you lost so much pay. So no one was late very often!

On your caps you'd only have 'HMS' because the name was blocked out – you weren't allowed to have your ship's name because

Janet Murray and friend, Hilda, with that rare commodity, fruit, courtesy of the Americans.

of the war. There's a little bow [on the cap ribbon] and everyone put a thrupenny bit in it – it must've been a tradition or something, but you pushed it in, so that you always had 3d on you. I remember at the end of the war, you had to hand your uniform in, and when I got home I was mad because I'd left my thrupenny bit in my cap!

In the build-up to D-Day, all leave was cancelled, and that was all we knew, but we had a feeling that something was brewing. Leslie, of course, was in the thick of that. We were married at the end of August 1944 and in November '44 he was shot down over Essen, and I got a telegram to say 'Your husband is missing'. I was on duty the next day and I remember I just had to carry on. Then, three days later, I got word that he'd landed safely in allied territory. It was a long three days, but somehow I felt he was alive. I don't know why; I just knew. I remember having to do this pay parade with an officer. The officers got their money paid into the bank, but the ratings got cash. We used to make up the pay with notes and florins, which were two shilling pieces. They used to come up and salute, hold their hat out and the pay was put on the hat. Then they'd salute again and go out. It was a right palaver! But my mind wasn't on it, of course, but [Leslie] got back all right in the end.

On VE Day, everybody was elated and they threw an impromptu dance and they were all piling into it – just the services; they didn't allow any civilians. I enjoyed myself in the Wrens. We had a lot of fun.

Petty Officer MR

Miss MR, a librarian by profession, joined the WRNS in 1942 and was posted to Gayhurst in Northampton, which was an outstation of the Bletchley Park codebreaking establishment. She worked with the Bombes which were used to decode German Enigma messages.

The morning after war broke out I was down at the recruiting office, because I wanted to do my bit. My father had been in the previous war, and I couldn't have faced people after the war, people who had lost relatives, if I hadn't done something. In any case, I was running a library, but there was really nothing to do. But the recruiting people wouldn't look at me: I couldn't drive, I couldn't type and I couldn't cook, so they sent me away.

At the end of the First World War, the Quaker Ambulance Unit had some money over and they founded a club in London.[7] It wasn't exclusively Quaker; certainly in 1939, they were very keen to get residents, providing you were in reasonable agreement with their beliefs. (They were extremely tolerant when I used to go back to the club in uniform. I got the same welcome as people who'd come out of prison for refusing to fire watch.) It was a lovely place, especially when some of the chaps who were in the universities were called up to work in the government. It was like a Senior Common Room, and I enjoyed it. I remember one occasion when we were all turned out of the club in the early hours of the morning because they wanted to carry an unexploded bomb from Bloomsbury Square to Russell Square. The more affluent went to hotels. I'd been running a library [not far away], and I said to my friends that I was going round to the library to sleep on the floor of the President's room, because that was the only room that had a carpet. So a few of us went round there, and I rang up the Registrar, Dr B., and told him we'd moved in because we'd been turned out of the Club. He asked whether the housekeepers were looking after us and I said Yes, that Mrs P. was providing tea and Mrs Williams was providing shaving water. 'Oh,' said Dr B., 'there are gentlemen in the party!' so I held my breath and said, 'Yes'. (He always looked straight-laced, but he wasn't as straight-laced as he seemed.) He said, 'How many?' and I said, 'There are four men and three girls', to which he replied, 'There aren't enough girls to go round!' One of the chaps snored terribly and he kept us awake much more than the bombs!

On 10 May, 1941, there was one of the last really big raids on London. For some reason, I was alone in the basement of the club, because we were sleeping in the basement on mattresses, and it was one of the few occasions I was really scared. I was alone in the basement right under the water pipes and I thought if we were hit I was going to be drowned. Anyway, in the morning I went round to see if I still had a library and as I walked in, I met my library ceiling coming down the stairs in a torrent of water. We hadn't been hit, but some of the buildings in the square had and the burning embers had dropped on our flat lead roof. Of course, the fire brigade did more damage than the fire, really – books don't burn easily, but they hate getting wet! I always think of that on May 10 now.

The streets of London were a mess. There were gaps where buildings had been, the rubble was cleared away fairly quickly. We had to move about in the blackout, which was a bit difficult because of the sandbags. I remember carrying a shaded torch, and finding it very difficult to walk in the dark without hitting something or someone. The first months of the Blitz were awful and very depressing. But our spirits were lifted as soon as the anti-aircraft barrage started up because we felt somebody was doing something about it. It was very curious because you'd hear the siren, and you'd think, 'Have I got time to wash out a pair of stockings before they start dropping things?' When I went down the odd time to my parents' home outside Eastbourne, I found it hard to sleep because it was so quiet; so I used to take the kitchen clock upstairs to break [the silence].

Eventually, with a general call-up of women coming into effect in 1942. Miss MR was sent for . . .

I believe it was Churchill who said, 'We need more girls on these machines', so in 1942, they found my file and called me up. I wasn't actually at Bletchley Park, I was at an outstation in Gayhurst, which was a lovely Elizabethan manor, but it had Elizabethan standards of comfort! I was caught badly by an age difference – all the girls were about 17, and I was 27, and that's an unbridgeable gap at that age. They all wanted to meet a nice young man and settle down; I wanted to finish my evening classes' degree course and get a better job; and I certainly didn't want to marry and have a family. I volunteered for the WRNS because the family tradition was seafaring, but I expect I would have been equally uncomfortable anywhere else! I'm not cut out for service life. Of course, for all these youngsters, it was wonderful. They'd left boarding school, and they felt it was freedom, but I'd left home at least seven years before and it wasn't the same for me at all. It wasn't their fault; it was just a question of background, and the age gap. The Wrens, as you can imagine, was a terrible culture shock – it was nobody's fault; it just happened.

Gayhurst was in the middle of nowhere and there was absolutely nothing to do when you were off watch, especially in the winter. The nearest civilisation was Newport Pagnell but there was no transport. We didn't seem to come into the provenance of NAAFI, but I don't remember much about the food, so it can't have been too bad! By then, Birkbeck College evening classes were moved to weekends so I got myself moved on educational grounds, to another outstation, at Stanmore, which at least was at the end of the Tube. I didn't manage to get up to Birkbeck, but at least I got up to see some friends and have some adult conversation!

Luckily I became a Petty Officer in 1945 and they couldn't retrain me for the Japanese war without my permission, and they certainly didn't get it! I'd had quite enough of service life – I was never alone; no privacy at all. Also, I had to sleep with my hand on my wallet [because of theft], which wasn't nice. I remember talking to somebody who'd just received a Postal Order; she put it down for a minute and it vanished. It wasn't a nice community to live in. Where we washed in the ablution block was a series of basins, and nowhere to put anything – you couldn't put your sponge or your soap or your towel anywhere; it was just the basin and the floor. After a bit, the bath taps lost their tops, so you couldn't turn them on, and you used to have a bath with your heel in the plughole, because there were no plugs. I had a spanner; I wouldn't lend it to anyone, but I'd go and turn the taps on for them, because that was the only way you could get a bath.

At Stanmore, I didn't enjoy sharing my bedroom with 49 other people. There were double-tiered, metal bunk beds, and you soon learnt not to choose the top one, because if somebody underneath was restless, it swayed. The [service] was playing at being sailors and these rooms were known as cabins.

We had a watch system: 8.00am to 4.00pm; 4.00pm to midnight; and midnight to 8.00am. It upset people, but it didn't upset my digestion as much as it did a lot of other people. The meals were so badly arranged. When you came off watch you needed a dinner, you didn't want breakfast, but the meals were geared to day watch. The other stupid thing was if day watch misbehaved, they were gated for the following week, but of course [by then], it was another lot of people, not the people who had sinned. So the new people, who hadn't done anything, were the ones who were gated! I must say I heard the word 'insubordination' quite often! If they told me to do something I thought was stupid, I'm afraid I said so. Another stupid thing was if, for some legitimate reason you weren't at Pay Parade, they didn't keep it; they sent it back, and it took about six weeks to get it again.

When I was on watch I was fitting these drums. They sent down a chart which was known as a menu, and told you how to align them. If you got them on, and got them right, and started the machine up, it printed something with the electric typewriter at the end, and stopped if it met something it was looking for. That was sent through to Bletchley, but I can't remember how. It must have gone by dispatch rider, because we put them into one of these suction things, like the system in drapers' shops, and they just disappeared. Very occasionally, we were told we'd managed to help somebody to break a code. You know, it was worth it! I was X service, and the machines were printing out what I presume Y service had picked up on the air. Y service were picking up the German signals. It was tied up with breaking the Enigma code and it was fascinating. I've learnt a lot more about it since I left, because, you see, we were just one little pocket [of the whole operation].

We had long periods on the night watch when there was nothing to do. I was in charge of a section, and I can remember getting a phone call: 'We've got a new assistant for you. I think she's the daughter of the Earl of X or something', and I said, 'Never mind, Ma'am, she may be quite nice'. That wasn't what they expected! Actually, she was; she was a very nice girl. We used to tease her and say, 'I suppose the second footman used to do that at home!' But there was an awful lot of snobbery.

I remember another incident in the Petty Officers' Mess. We had fish on Fridays, often followed by ice cream, but I needed something slightly more substantial for the second course. So I pushed my chair away from the table and announced, 'That was very nice. What time's tea?' The Petty Officer cook got up and walked out, and the others said, 'You've had it!' I said, 'Well, I'm going to be hungry in a few hours'. At any rate, she came back with a loaf of bread and cheese. I don't think that, for the young, ice cream on top of fish is enough for the main meal.

When I became a Petty Officer, it was great because I was allowed to wear leather gloves. I didn't like the knitted ones because the wind went through them, and they slipped on things, like when you were getting onto buses. But I've got broad hands, and I couldn't get into any of the store's leather gloves so they gave me a chit and I went to Liberty's in Regent Street and got a very nice pair! The other way I scored was because I'd always worn flat-heeled shoes. Most of the other girls were in agony because of their calves. Also I had worn a tie at school, and most of them hadn't, and because I couldn't tie a tie from the front, I spent a lot of time standing on a chair behind people, tying their ties from the back!

When I was off duty, I tried to read, but the light was so bad. I did try a correspondence course in political theory but it was just impossible in those circumstances. I seemed to have an awful lot of books with me but they always stayed on the bunk, and, of course, they had to go on the floor when I went to bed. We did get leave, but the married girls all got priority for leave, for when their husbands were home, which I suppose was fair enough, but it didn't go down terribly well. We got a travel warrant [for leave], and I had a bit of trouble there. They always made the travel warrant out for your home address but I wasn't going home; I was going back to where I was living in London and where all my friends were. Anyway, I got it sorted out; they automatically thought you were going home, but I wasn't.

After the war, we weren't demobbed, we were released; and my release was held up for several days because they had to count my teeth! They hadn't counted them when I went in, so I suppose it was just one of those things. I had enjoyed the Blitz — in those days, I preferred to be frightened than bored! I look back on those years as the most miserable I have ever spent. I felt no sense of comradeship and made no friends. I do not regret those three miserable years but enjoyment was not the object of the exercise.

Ordinary Wren Doris Watson

Ordinary Wren Doris Watson joined up in 1943, when she was 21 years old. She came from Newcastle upon Tyne, and she had just married Leslie, who was serving in the RAF. She was a teleprinter operator, taking down the Germans' encrypted messages transmitted by their Enigma machine, and then sending them to Bletchley Park.

When I joined, I went to Mill Hill in London, which was a sorting-out centre. I was there for a fortnight, and then we had to go and do some training. I was a pretty quick and accurate typist and I think that got me to what I did — it was [with] Enigma. I was based at

Scarborough and we were in digs at first but the main headquarters
was the Hotel Cecil. We used to go there for our breakfast, or supper
if you were on night duty, then we'd get the bus up to the place
where they intercepted the [German] messages. We were just lowly
little teleprinter operators so we didn't count for much! It was the
[people] down at Bletchley . . . who were absolutely fantastic at
deciphering the [messages], and, of course, the Germans didn't
know – they were happily sending the messages out.

When we were on watch, we used to do so many hours during the day, then you got a couple of days off, then so many hours at night. We were in the teleprinter room where there was a row of teleprinters and there were mostly local girls in there, who had joined up when [it] started. We had lots of fun. The [girls] who took the messages had earphones on, and they sat and listened to all this stuff coming through. There was a lot of interference – you got a lot of broken [signals]. You know – there were four letters [for example], and sometimes you just got three, or two. We had to go from where we were [in the teleprinter room] along to the sparks room, where the [girls] sat with earphones on. There was always a pile of messages and you had to pick these up and run back with them. Then they got spread out among the teleprinter operators so we could send them through to Bletchley on the teleprinters, which were just like a typewriter.

In the build-up to D-Day, my husband was given 48 hours' leave to come home. I was on night shift, and I went off because I'd got [a] message to say I could go, because he'd got this pass to come up and see me. One of the girls who lived there had to go in [to take] my place and she wasn't very [pleased]; in fact, she was most upset about it. So I was up with the captain, but he was very nice [about it]. He said, 'When do you expect to see your husband again?' and I said I didn't know; because I didn't – it was just before D-Day. And he said, 'The trouble is, they shouldn't send married women to this place.' so that was all I got – it was all right; I got off with it, and I didn't get into trouble when I thought I might have done! After the leave I went back on duty, but we didn't really know what was going on – it wasn't until afterwards that we found out.

There was an increase in the German messages that were being intercepted in the build-up to D-Day, but Doris says they weren't aware of the British plans.

They didn't seem to know. We got one of their ships in the Mediterranean as a result of the messages. And we got a message through to thank us for the work we'd done.

There were times when we got desperately fed up because boyfriends and husbands were away, but at the same time we all just worked in together.

[Then] we had a big change around and we were sent to Winchester, still [doing] the same thing. We were there for a while, and then it was VE Day and I was home [in Newcastle] for that – I'd been demobbed. That was exciting because we had parties. I remember one of the [British] prisoners of war came back, and they had a tremendous welcome for him. All the poor lad wanted to do was go home and go to bed. He just didn't want to be made a fuss of.

And on V J Day, you were glad it was all over.

Leading Wren 375? Pamela Weightman

Pamela Weightman was an administrator in Newcastle upon Tyne, in the executive council offices, dealing with the issuing of medical cards, payment of doctors and chemists, etc. until she joined up in 1941 at the age of 19. In the WRNS, she became a plotter.

A view of the plotting room. Note the earphones on the Wren in the foreground; this was how the girls received the plots that were to be transferred to the map on the table.

For the first year and few months after I joined up, I lived at home and trained at the plot in the Central Exchange in Newcastle. The real plot was in Askham House in Gosforth [Newcastle] and I went there eventually. I knew straight away I was going to be a plotter – I think they were training plotters ready for the invasion. The plots used to come in from a radar station – they were all up the coast and mainly run by the air force but there were naval people attached to them – and there was a Cassini grid out on a table, a chart in squares, and each square had a number and two letters. The plots would come in and you had to work out where they should go on the grid, and then you got the spot where the boat was. The plots were of anything that was going up or down the coast. We had headphones on and the radar stations used to send the plots to us every quarter of an hour, transmitted through the headphones.

After about 18 months, I was posted to Portsmouth to train others how to plot; this was early in 1943. There was lots of things to do on your time off. There were NAAFIs to go to and we had free rein to go wherever we liked, but once the invasion started, we didn't. Orchestras used to come down and we had concerts. My friend, Renie, and I used to hitch lifts when we stayed at each other's home. This man picked us up one time. He was in civvies but he turned out to be a naval officer. He didn't believe in Wrens hitching – it was not the thing for Wrens to do! So he put us out at a station – I don't know where it was – and bought us tickets to go to London. Another time we got a lift and it was in a funny little car that was like a truck with the seats in the front and an open back. We got in with the man and he told us that Fareham was on his way, and he'd been up to London selling pigs. He told us we'd have to make a detour because he had to see somebody, so we stopped in front of this hotel. He told us to go into the dining room and he went off, where to I don't know; and they came and served us a meal, and it was lovely. We hadn't ordered it. Eventually we got back into the car when he was ready to go, and when we got to Fareham, he put us out. He was getting our bags out and before he left we thanked him and offered to pay for the meal. 'Oh no, no, no – that's mine; I've paid for that', and then he gave each of us £1. When we got back to quarters, the Petty Officer told us we'd missed the paying out and that she'd go and get it for us – every so often she used to pay out [some money] from the funds – and she gave us another £1! When we told her about the man, we got a real telling off for getting in with him.

The main reason we went [to Portsmouth] was because we plotted individually. Most plotters would plot in a mass, because of convoys, but we did the plots separately. We were taken to the dockyard, where the plot was so secret that we had to go up in twos; I can't see the point in it, but we did that. They were so glad to see us that one of the other girls and I were put directly onto night watch. The plot was in Fort Southwick but we were billeted further down the road in Fort Wallington. They were Napoleonic forts and built into the hill so you just saw the door on the outside.

I was there for the build-up to D-Day and all through the invasion. We could see where all the LCTs were, and wagonloads of the army used to come in to go to the LCTs. There were all these

**The plotting room where Leading Wren Pamela Weightman
plotted the movements on the Channel during D–Day and before.**

funny tanks with chains at the front and we didn't know what they
were for. There was lots of extra traffic going through. This all went
on for quite a while beforehand. I was on watch on the night of D–
Day. We were told that it was happening, but it was top secret. It was
put off because the weather was bad. They said we'd be going down
into the tunnel but they didn't know whether we'd be coming up
the same day or not, if anything had happened, if the Germans had
retaliated. This tunnel was 150 feet [45.72m] below the ground
beneath Fort Southwick and everybody worked in there; it was
headquarters and all the operations worked from there. When [the
invasion] started, we were signalled that they'd gone, so we had to
pick up the plots from the radar stations, and then track them across.
We couldn't plot them individually this time because there were so
many. I wasn't plotting; I had to stand at the front of the table and

watch the plotters and be ready for any queries that cropped up. We had officers, and air force, the fleet air arm as well, all standing up the stairs overlooking it [see photograph]. We used to stick these little [tokens] for the ships into small blocks of wood and move them on the grid. As soon as they'd landed at the other side, we got a signal to say the troops had landed. When I came off watch the next morning, the gliders and aeroplanes were still going over. The Wren going on watch said, 'Ooh, something must be going to happen today because they're getting ready for it.' I said, 'No. It's happened. They're there!'

After D-Day, they were bringing the LCTs back because they were empty now. It was terrible weather and a signal went out that they were not to be sent back, it was dangerous if one got loose and was floating about in the Channel. Well, the Americans said, 'We don't listen to things like that. We can do that'. So they brought some back. Of course, some did get loose and for a long time afterwards there were LCTs popping up in the Channel. The boats that were out there looking for them were popping them and sinking them.

We knew it was important but it was just our job and we got on with it. I enjoyed my time very much and I never regretted joining up.

King George VI visiting the plotting room just after D–Day. Leading Wren Pamela Weightman was present.

Ordinary Wren 55232 Audrey Bell

Audrey Bell did not see war service, as she was just a little too young to join up when there was a need for women in the services. However, she joined the WRNS immediately after the end of the war, when the whole of Europe was totally wrecked. She was posted to Germany, where she witnessed at first hand the devastation wrought by six years of conflict.

I left school at 16 and went to work in the local council offices as a junior clerk. In the summer of 1946 there was an advert in the paper looking for Wrens because the [wartime] girls were due to be demobbed, and that was how I got in.

I went to Burghfield [near Reading] and did my basic training and then I went to Portsmouth to do my signal training; and then we got posted to Germany. I went to Hamburg and had a fabulous time out there. The navy was left in Germany after the war to clear the docks and the seaports, because they were bombed and damaged. There were the U-boat pens on the River Elbe that were all broken up. I was there when there was the bombing of Heligoland[8] when they blew it up.

We were posted into a big barracks. The severe winter of '46/'47 it was bitter cold and we had no coal or anything. We were in these beautiful modern barracks built for the Luftwaffe, and survived the cold by wrapping up well. We realised how stark everything was. There were miles and miles of devastation and no trees, because they'd either been blown up or chopped down to use for firewood.

They were pulling the forces out of Germany to turn it over to the German government, to give them the rule of the country again, so they closed down the barracks that I was in. But they left a few of us behind; there were ten Wrens left to show the white ensign,[9] and we were attached to an army barracks. We did our usual signals work, messages and so on. The signals were between the Admiralty in London and Berlin, decoding messages; it was all hush-hush work.

We were there when the Russians closed the borders between East and West, and from the house where we were, on the banks of the river, we overlooked the flying boats taking off every day to take the supplies to Berlin.[10] They were taking coal and flour, and everything up there. We entertained the RAF pilots who were

flying the flying boats and had a bit of life there, until the time came when we had to go back to England.

We had [German civilian] staff working for us. We had two lovely ladies and a German man driver. If you tried to discuss the war with them, they wouldn't discuss it with you at all. They were very, very down-and-out, and very grateful for any cast-offs we gave them. They had young children who didn't have any shoes, and they were so grateful for anything that we gave them.

Going out into the city, there were miles and miles of devastation – it was all rubble that was left [from the bombing]. They had no equipment really – not the mechanical equipment we had – they had wheelbarrows; and with their bare hands, the women and children and the men who were available were clearing away the rubble, putting it into the wheelbarrows and taking it away so they could start rebuilding.

Most of the older houses had cellars, and there was a black cross painted on the [wall] to show there were bodies in the cellars. What they did, I don't know; whether they just sealed them up or what . . .

They were just getting back onto their feet again. There was the old-fashioned trolley things – the services had their own transport, of course – and the boats; Hamburg's got canals, so they used the boats. The shops were very, very few and far between, and not a lot in them.

It was an in-between time because the forces were still there, so all the bigger hotels were taken over by [them]. We had one where there was a NAAFI and we could go there at night and have a meal. That was where we did our courting! We went out and had a meal together. I can remember I used to love the tinned liver in lovely thick, rich gravy with onions. It was like a holiday camp for us. The officers would come in from their camps in the surrounding districts. They'd ring up the Wrenery and say, 'We're coming in for a night on the town. Are any of the girls free to join us?' and they would take us for a night out. We managed to get leave and I went down to Brussels and Paris, and skiing up in the Alps where Hitler had his retreat in Bavaria. They were just beginning to open up again, like the Opera House – I remember going to a ballet. The British Forces Network was there, and they used to put on concerts for the troops.[11]

I can remember one night going to a concert and there was *Two-way Family Favourites* with Cliff Michelmore and Jean Metcalfe.[12] Cliff Michelmore was working in Germany – he was in an Air Force uniform – and he spoke up, 'Is there an Audrey Bell in the audience?' I put my hand up and he said, 'Come and see me after the performance.' I'd written in a request because my husband-to-be was back in England by that time, and [Cliff Michelmore] said he was going to play a record for me on the Sunday, so I was able to notify them at home. But he didn't play the record of my choice!

1   King George VI, Queen Elizabeth and Princesses Elizabeth and Margaret paid an official visit to South Africa from February to May 1947. Shortly after their return, Princess Elizabeth announced her engagement to Prince Phillip Mountbatten of Greece.

2   For more information on LCTs see http://en.wikipedia.org/wiki/landing_craft_tank

3   Ann Sheridan was an American film actress. For more information see http://en.wikipedia.org/wiki/ann_sheridan

4   The bombe was an electromechanical device used by British cryptologists to help break German Enigma-machine-generated signals during World War II. For more information, see http://en.wikipedia.org/wiki

5   The Enigma machine encrypted the German messages which, unknown to them, were intercepted and forwarded to the personnel at Bletchley Park, who cracked the code. For more information. see http://bletchleypark.org.uk/content/hist/wartime.rhtm

6   For more information on HMS Starling, see http://uboat.net/allies/warships/ship/3948html

7   For more information about the Penn Club see http://pennclub.co.uk

8   For more information about Heligoland, see http://en.wikipedia.org/wiki/heligoland

9   For more information`see http://en.wikipedia.org/wiki/white_ensign

10 The Berlin blockade (June 1948-May1949) was one of the first major international crises of the cold war. The Western Allies organised the Berlin airlift to carry supplies to the people in West Berlin. For more information, see http://en.wikipedia.org/wiki/berlin_blockade

11 For more information, see http://n.wikipedia.org/wiki/british_forces_broadcasting_service

12 Two-way Family Favourites was a popular radio show that linked the British forces in Germany with their loved ones at home. It was presented by Cliff Michelmore and Jean Metcalfe, who eventually married. For more information, see http://www.whirligig-tv.co.uk/radio/twff.htm

Chapter 4

They Also Serve . . .

. . . but the following women did not stand and wait, by any means. Farming, nursing, fire fighting, working with chemicals for the war effort – all these occupations were carried out by the women who are featured in this chapter. As the war went on, and more men were called up to the front, their jobs had to be done by the women left behind. Here, we'll read about the amazing experiences some of those women had.

Women's Land Army – WLA

The Women's Land Army (WLA) was a civilian organisation created by the Board of Agriculture in 1915, in which women worked in agriculture, replacing the men who were called up to the armed forces. Women who worked for the WLA were commonly known as 'Land Girls', and were sent to farms that were short of workers, the farmers being their employers. With six million men away fighting, Britain was struggling for labour, so women were encouraged to become involved in the production of food, and do their part to support the war effort. Towards the end of 1917, there were over 250,000 women working as farm labourers.

As the prospect of a second world war became increasingly likely, the government realised the importance of growing food within Britain. In order to increase productivity, more help was needed on the farms and so the Women's Land Army was started again in June 1939. Although under the control of the Ministry of Agriculture and Fisheries, it was given an honorary head in Lady Gertrude Denman. At first it asked for volunteers, but membership was then supplemented by conscription. By 1944, it had over 80,000 women working in agriculture and forestry. The WLA lasted until its official disbandment on 21 October, 1950.

A related organisation, the Women's Timber Corps, worked in the forestry industry, and its members were known as 'Lumber Jills'.

Miss Dorothea Abbott, WLA 104076

Dorothea Abbott was a pacifist and, as such, she preferred not to join any of the armed services, so she enrolled with the Women's Land Army. At the age of 22, she received orders to report to the Women's Land Army Hostel at the Manor House, Nether Feldon, Warwickshire, in October 1942. A librarian by profession, she was to be thrown into a life totally new, but not unwelcome, since she was pleased enough to leave her work in the reference library in Birmingham.

> The manor house was built in grey stone, in pseudo-Gothic style, in the heart of Shakespeare's Warwickshire. Mrs Coker ('Cokey') was the warden and she took me to a bedroom on the first floor. There were six beds and the one that was pushed across the fireplace in an ideal position to catch all the draughts from the chimney was mine! She left me to unpack my uniform. There was a fawn drill milking coat and dungarees, two aertex shirts, six pairs of thick woollen socks, canvas gaiters as a substitute for gumboots, and the green jersey, khaki breeches and black boots which were the walking-out uniform of the Land Army. I was disappointed to find the greatcoat missing. After several attempts at viewing myself in the dressing table mirror, I decided that breeches did nothing at all for my behind!
>
> Clothing was rationed, and all our garments had to be literally worn out before being discarded. The *Land Girl* magazine was constantly advocating new uses for old shirts, such as conversion to briefs to be worn under dungarees, or cutting up for face flannels! We were issued with six pairs of Land Army stockings and one might almost say they were our Achilles' heel. More than any other topic, this cropped up again and again in the correspondence columns of the *Land Girl*, how to prolong the life of these thick woollen stockings until we were allowed to apply for some more.
>
> Darning was a hated chore, and we invented many devices to avoid it. One hardy Suffolk volunteer didn't wear socks at all, having found her boots so comfortable. Other [people] knitted their own

stockings from oiled sea-boot wool. Re-footing and patching were comparatively simple solutions, but there was a girl from Kent who sewed little wash-leather shields into the toes and heels of hers.

The 'Make Do and Mend' campaign was at its height in the middle years of the war, and people nowadays who have known only the affluent society will have difficulty imagining even a Land Girl writing to a magazine to say she'd made knitted shirts out of non-rationed dish cloth yarn, that they washed well, and in time became quite white! From time to time, official instructions on the care of uniform appeared. We were told to put a bag of sawdust in our hat to help it keep its shape; and after a day's work in wet weather, to stuff our boots with hay and straw. We were told that both boots and shoes would need breaking in, and that we mustn't mind if the boots in particular felt hard at first. To which advice we were tempted to reply, 'Stuff it'! Problems like aching backs, blisters, and trying to protecting your eyes when threshing [were all discussed] in the pages of the *Land Girl*. They advised us to mix grated carrots and lard, warm it in the oven and allow it to set, as a cure for chilblains; and recommended a salve [farmers] used for cows' udders to keep our hands soft. A rotten tomato apparently worked wonders for removing tomato stains from the hands!

Near Christmas, we planned a party in the village hall and we decided to do it in style. We invited the Pioneers[1] and the boys from the Air Force camp. We raided our mothers' larders and came back with jellies, mincemeat, sugar, biscuits and other delicacies that were either rationed or in short supply. The party was fixed for the Wednesday and on the Monday, we woke to lashing rain, and we were thrilled knowing there'd be no work that day. After breakfast, we tidied the hostel and prepared the vegetables for the evening meal, and in the afternoon we went down to the village hall armed with brooms, mops, buckets and dusters. We worked hard and I wished my mother could have seen me – she'd have been surprised at such enthusiasm, because at home I was only interested in getting out of the housework! By tea time the decorations were up, and the [only] piece of mistletoe was placed in a strategic position by the door. A bus ran twice a day from Feldon to Stratford and some of the girls had made the journey on the afternoon bus, hoping to buy cakes for the party. Stratford was well supplied with cake shops, and by queueing at different ones in turn they had done reasonably well.

Since joining the WLA, food had taken a much more important place in my life. I had acquired an enormous appetite from working outside at hard manual work, and was always hungry. (When I came home at weekends, I used to scrounge what dripping there was from our meagre joint, spread it on bread, and eat slice after slice. My mother said it made her feel sick.) So, not least among the attractions of the party were the eats! There was plenty of food. I hadn't seen so many colourful jellies and blancmanges since a friend's 21st birthday party soon after the outbreak of war. Our family wasn't well supplied with friends or relatives in the food trade, and what we had was strictly on ration. It was obvious from looking at the loaded table that some of the girls must've had friends in the right quarters! The supper was for me one of the highlights of the evening. Men were in plentiful supply too, with a party of sergeants over from the Mess, and there were airmen, Pioneers and local lads.

Everyone enjoyed that party. We got a huge kick from dressing up for it, and the bathrooms smelled like beauty parlours. Most of us lived in slacks in the evenings, and as a visit to the Sergeants' Mess or a dance at The Hut involved a long cycle ride on a cold evening, we tended to wear our walking-out uniform of greatcoat, green jersey and best gabardine breeches. Consequently, we'd never seen each other dressed up, and some of the transformations were quite remarkable. One of the girls surprised me the next day by saying, 'You did look lovely last night, Dorothy [sic], in that yellow dress and your cheeks like two rosy apples'.

One of our first jobs in the New Year was sprout-picking. At eight o'clock on a grey morning, a field of Brussels sprouts is about as cheerful as a cemetery. We had to pick the sprouts from the bottom of the stalk, working upwards, and put them into nets. There were six girls from the hostel, working with two men from the farm. While we were still warm from our ride [to the farm, on our bikes], it was tolerable but we soon cooled off. We'd prance about getting warm and our breath would spiral up in the frosty air. When the sun started to break through, it added to our troubles. While the sprouts were hard and frosty it was easier to pick them off, but as they started to melt, the wet soaked through our gloves and numbed our fingers. They felt stiff and useless, and we envied the farm workers who could peel off several sprouts at once! I remember I began to feel queer – I'd never been very clever at coping with cold and I hoped I wasn't going to pass out. My fingers were tingling. It was a quarter past ten and we knew tea would be coming soon, but I felt detached and the conversation around me came from a long way away. Light years later, it seemed, came the hum of a tractor and there was the farmer with a basket of cups and a jug of tea. I gulped mine down gratefully – it seemed heaven-sent, and to think that I used not to drink it! The farmer loaded our nets of sprouts onto the trailer and drove off. I'd look at a dish of Brussels sprouts after that with more respect. I was reminded of the Land Army Christmas card with the verse, 'Be gentle when you touch bread . . .'

One spring, Dorothea was offered the chance to transfer to a poultry farm, to take charge of the stock there. She was ready for a change and so jumped at the opportunity. She learned many new skills as the poultry maid at Over Feldon Farm, which was owned by Mr and Mrs Seal.

We usually collected the eggs in the middle of the morning, in a basket. I used to open the nest boxes from the outside and ease my hand under the sitting hens. Eggs come out soft but within seconds of meeting the air they solidify. Some of the hens seemed to be very bad tempered, squawking and even pecking my hand. Fowl aren't really likeable creatures, brainless enough to bite the hand that feeds them. I'd collect the eggs, brown and white, and take them into the scullery, to put into wooden packing cases, ready for the packing station at Henley-in-Arden. They collected [the eggs] once a week. My first job after lunch every day was to wash the eggs, because they didn't pay as much for dirty ones. The hens were Light Sussex and Rhode Island Reds, and they used to congregate around the gates to their runs, on the lookout for food. We used to feed them with their wet mash mixed with potatoes which had been boiled in Bertie the Boiler. Bertie was quite a problem. On the days when the Boss was at home, Bertie would roar away; when I was on my own, he would smoulder sullenly and even go out. They also had a gander on the farm that used to hiss menacingly as people went past. I used to shout, 'Get off, you bugger!' in my best Land Army manner, when I met him – he could do quite a lot of damage with his serrated beak, and he didn't seem to have altogether taken to me.

If we were getting in some chicks, we had to get the brooder house ready, so Mr Seal would bring a drum of oil up from the village so we could light the lamps and get the place warm. I had to scatter peat litter around, from a large bale, and it needed to be changed every day. I'd fill the hoppers with dry chick mash, and give it to the chicks every two hours for the first three days. I had to put all the food troughs away at night, to avoid encouraging rats.

I remember once going with Mr Seal to collect some chicks from the railway station. The chicks had been put on the train near Evesham and were in four cardboard boxes. They were surprisingly light, and each one contained fifty cheeping chickens. We rushed them back to the brooder house and unloaded fifty into each hover[2] and then shut them up to keep warm. A couple were already dead, trampled by the others. I was thrilled by their appearance – two hundred tiny balls of yellow fluff; they looked just like decorations for Easter eggs. It didn't matter if they didn't have anything to eat because there's enough nourishment from the egg to last 48 hours.

We went for a cup of tea and Mr Seal's farmhand, old Joe, was in the kitchen complaining about 'they dratted birds'. We suddenly heard a loud peeping from the brooder house and Mrs Seal asked me to go and see what was the matter. Well, I set off hastily, and caught a basket of four dozen eggs with the toe of my boot. There was a crash as they scattered all over the garden path; yolks and shells everywhere in one glutinous mess! Eggs were expensive at that time of year and I was worried what Mrs Seal would say, but I could see she was struggling between vexation and the desire to laugh. As I was bending to pick up the few unbroken eggs that had survived, I heard Joe say, 'Her's the clumsiest bloody sod as ever I seed'!

Anyway, I went to the brooder house and noticed that the chicks had become more active, and most of them were scratching in the peat and feeding. While this was going on, there was a lot of squawking and grumbling from the hens in the nest boxes. One of the Light Sussex had pounced on a broken egg and had taken a good beakful. I was shocked as I had no idea fowl were such cannibalistic creatures. Over a few days the chicks would grow, their wing and tail feathers became distinguishable, and they lost their first endearing fluffiness. They were very lively, clamouring for their food if I kept them waiting, and even clambering all over my hands when I put the food hoppers down. When a week had passed without more casualties I felt that I would safely rear them after all.

One afternoon I heard an extraordinary sound. It was as though all the fowl were murmuring in panic, and it was accompanied by the whirring of wings, and through the fruit trees I could see several fluttering about. Mrs Seal and I hurried through the goose run and looked around. There was a trail of white feathers which led to the covert, and the hens were still sending up alarm cries. Behind a hen house I found a Light Sussex, with its gory neck lying beside it. Mrs Seal shouted from the fence near the covert, 'This is where he's been lying,' and when I joined her I was hit by the most appalling smell. That's what's meant by the scent of a fox. Well, it was boiled fowl for lunch the next day. He'd got away with another, too, judging by all the feathers that were lying around. That was my first experience of the violence done by foxes, and although I didn't agree with fox-hunting, I had to admit they were a menace.

Mrs Seal suggested I try my hand at plucking and dressing the dead fowl because it would be good practice for my Proficiency Badge. The WLA had recently instituted Proficiency Tests in various branches of farming. If you were taking the Poultry Test, you had to kill, pluck and dress a fowl, and speed was taken into account. I was keen to enter, but I thought I needed a lot more practice. Anyway, at least the fox had made the first part of the test unnecessary! The following morning, I settled down in the brooder house with a sack round my waist and a bucket for the feathers. I jumped when I heard 'Morning, Dorothy', and it was old Joe looking at me with amusement. He said, 'How be you a gettin' on?' and I told him I was doing a lot in a long time, to which he replied, 'You want to dip that old hen in boiling water. All they feathers will come off a treat.' Now, I'd read that that method was frowned upon in all the best poultry circles, so I just said the Boss had told me how to do it, and he snorted. It was fortunate that we were having our main meal at night because my fowl would never have been ready for lunch. If I stripped the feathers off too fast, I tore the flesh, which is another thing not done in the best poultry circles. After an endless time, I was able to hang up the plucked carcase and singe off the whiskers with a lighted newspaper. Then I had to extract the innards. Mrs Seal gave me a demonstration – she was fearful she'd never get the bird in the pot at all if the dressing was left entirely to me. In the end, I decided I wouldn't be in too much of a hurry to take that Proficiency Test!

I remember when one of the geese was sitting. The gander swelled with pride as he stood guard over her, and he was fiercer than ever – he had many a skirmish with the labrador, who always got the worst of it. One morning I could hear the goslings beginning to tap their way through their shells. The goose had been a devoted mother; she sat for 30 days and scarcely left the nest, even to feed. After the goslings had hatched, they dried off and were bright green. It was the first time I'd seen young goslings, and they were absolutely enchanting. The Boss didn't know who was the proudest of those six goslings: the goose, the gander or me! I loved standing in the goose run watching them feed. They'd shovel the sloppy mash all over their green fluff, and I'd have given them bibs if I could – it was a shame for them to get so bedraggled.

During the spring I had to collect the eggs four times a day as there was such a glut. I loved an egg for tea – there's nothing to compare with a fresh egg laid by a hen on free range. The cock used to sidle up to me and was really belligerent. He'd poke his head forward and make little darting runs at me. I'd shout, 'You bugger off!' [to make him back away]. But I'd forgive the cockerel all his aggressiveness just to hear the wonderful ring to his cry in the early mornings, as opposed to the sleepy sound of wood pigeons.

Every Saturday I used to hitch a lift on a gravel lorry and spend the day in Stratford. I'd come back on the last bus which was at 8.30pm. The lorry drivers would always stop for anyone in uniform, and I usually carried a few eggs which I'd leave behind in the driving cab. They were decent types, and I only once had any trouble, when the driver pulled in at the side of the road and said, 'Give us a kiss, love.' I refused, of course, and so he lay down with his head in my lap, and said, 'Right! I'm staying here until you do'. I contemplated taking an egg out of my bag and cracking it on his forehead, but decided against it. So I just sat there looking out of the window pretending to take no notice. Then he said, 'I could stay here all day,' but a moment later there was a hoot from the driver of another gravel lorry pulling in behind, and 'my' driver sat up. He started his engine and said, 'Some of you girls have hearts of stone.'

I always wandered round the Stratford shops before lunch, usually buying a book, because there weren't any libraries near Feldon. In those days, because of rationing and scarcity, there wasn't much else you could buy, and books were comparatively cheap. After lunch I'd go to the theatre, and buy a balcony ticket at the door for under two shillings. That's how I saw most of Shakespeare and by the end of my three years in the district there were few of the plays I hadn't seen. To fortify myself and to fill in the time, I'd have two teas at different shops, but the dainty afternoon teas they served were only appetising little snacks to me, and I was still ready for hot milk and biscuits when I returned to the farm.

I went home every month for a weekend, but I began to get tired of the long hilly ride back from Stratford on Sunday evenings. So when the Boss told me there was a notice in the grocer's window advertising an auto-cycle, I was more than interested. It was a Rudge[3], and did 125 miles to the gallon, or so the Boss told me! I wondered whether I could manage it, but the Boss said there was nothing to it. The clutch and throttle controls were on the handlebars, and they could be switched off if you're in difficulties; and you used the pedals like an ordinary bicycle. So I raided my bank account and although the £30 made a hole in my savings, it was wonderful to have my own transport.

The Boss gave me a crash course on the front drive, and the next evening I set off for Compton Wynyates, feeling like Toad and his motor-car![4]

It was a perfect evening, and I sailed effortlessly up the hills. I felt a new person. Compton Wynyates was all I'd expected it to be, and when I started my bike [to go back] the engine gave a faint splutter and died. Well, I tinkered round with the controls, and checked the petrol, and wondered what I'd forgotten. There was nothing for it but to pedal all the way back, and the Boss soon identified the problem, a dirty sparking plug. So then I carried a spare for emergencies. Well, not long after that, the engine refused to start when I was on the outskirts of Stratford, and I decided the only thing I could do was wait on a slope until somebody passed by. The plan was to ask for a push, pedal down the hill and hope the engine would start before I got to the bottom. It was lunchtime and there wasn't a soul about, but eventually a tennis player came along, dressed in clean white flannels, and carrying his racquet. He wasn't the type I'd have chosen to ask, but I was desperate! He looked surprised, but I was in uniform and he obligingly ran behind me as I pedalled furiously and let in the clutch. The engine suddenly

Miss Dorothea Abbott on her Rudge autocycle.

jumped into life and I accelerated, and roared off, leaving my Sir Galahad flat in the dust!

Another great event was the killing of poor Tessie O'Shea[5], the sow. One morning she had to be left without breakfast, and soon afterwards Harry Smith arrived to lance her throat. I kept well out of the way of the pig killing, but even so the noise was indescribable and made me feel quite ill. The corpse was left to drain while we all adjourned for a cup of tea. Then [it was time to] joint the pig. My part in all this was to run backwards and forwards from the sty to the larder with buckets of offal and pig meat. Harry Smith carried the two sides and hams into the larder himself, and in no time he'd laid out the bacon and hams in the new wooden trough, rubbed in salt and coated them in black treacle. He sorted out the meat and offal and put it in enamel bowls accompanied by a running commentary: 'My Mam makes bony pies of this'; 'My Mam puts this aside for hot faggots'; 'She hoses the chitterlings through and uses the ears, tail and head for brawn'; 'The pig's feet make wonderful eating'. When it came to the leaf⁶, he waxed eloquent: 'My Mam chops this up to the size of lump sugar and simmers it all day to keep it white. It'll keep for a year, and the scratchings⁷ are lovely.'

Mrs Seal put the rest of the pig meat in pickle, and we feasted on pig's liver, faggots, chitterlings and trotters for the next few days. It wasn't all for our own use, because the Boss had several friends anxious to take some of it off his hands. The bacon and hams were left to cure, and for some time afterwards I hardly dared look the pigs in the face!

Miss Dorothea Abbott driving a tractor.

One Saturday I got back from Stratford to find that the water diviner had come, and after tramping all over the farm with a hazel twig, he'd struck water in the side orchard, not far from the turkey houses. He'd cut a forked hazel twig from the hedge and, holding it in both hands, palms uppermost, he'd walked up and down the front field and all over the orchards. The farmer was just beginning to think it wasn't going to work when the twig had suddenly reacted violently, tearing the skin off the diviner's hands.

Martin the builder and Bill, his mate, came to start digging the following week. Their equipment was amazingly simple: a couple of shovels, two buckets, a jack, a winch and some rope. I was picking Bramley apples and Conference pears near the site of the well, so I was a constant spectator. First they dug a hole in the ordinary way, standing in it and throwing spadesful of earth above the surface. Bill was a bricklayer by trade, and he added a lining of bricks as they went down. This sank under its own weight with only a little assistance from the jack. They struck clay in the afternoon, and they let down a short ladder, and they took turns digging and carrying the earth up. Every day the hole grew deeper and the ladder was changed for longer ones. Martin kept measuring with his plumb and spirit level to make sure they were digging a true course. Ten feet [3m] below ground and there was still no sign of water! Eventually Martin and Bill were winding each other up and down in a bucket, a laborious business. Then Martin invited me to have a ride down in the bucket, which was a challenge! When I touched down, Bill showed me around [the well bottom] which was five feet [1.5m] in diameter. He picked up some dampish clay which he reckoned meant they were nearly there. I thought going back up wouldn't be so bad, but that's where I was wrong. I'd been wound up only a little way when the bucket began spinning round violently. I was feeling sick, and going up very slowly because I was no light weight for Martin to wind, boots and all. The bucket was still revolving and I felt so dizzy I was afraid I'd fall out. It was one of the few moments of panic I'd ever experienced.

Forty feet [12m] down they struck water. It seemed strangely silent when the well diggers had gone, leaving behind them a permanent water supply.

By the time I was demobbed, I'd been in the district for over three years. I went round saying goodbye to my friends. They were such real people, and when I was leaving them, I knew I was saying goodbye to a vanishing way of life – the days of the small farm were numbered.

(The above account was adapted, with the very kind permission of Dorothea Abbott, from *Librarian in the Land Army*, ISBN 0 9509 3960 9)

Miss Kit Knox

Kit (Catherine) Knox joined the Land Army in 1942 when she was just 18 years old. She had previously been with the YWCA, which had been looking after the Land Army girls in their hostels. Kit decided that if those girls could manage the work, then so could she! She was hoping she would get a place similar to those girls, working in a market garden, but it wasn't to be.

I was assigned to Mr Shepherd, doing general farm work, in Sadberge near Darlington [County Durham]. It was the only farm in that small village, and they had cows, horses, one bull. There were two men who looked after the cattle; and I was assigned to milk the cows. You had to clean out the byres so they were clean when the cows came in. They seemed to know which individual stall they were to go into, and you'd already put food in there for them to eat, and the water came by – they'd just push in their heads and they got a drink that way. You had to wrap your arms around the neck of the cow to chain them in; they kept on throwing their heads up, which I was a bit nervous about at first. Then you had to wash the udders and then start to milk by hand. Now, the farmer told me you can't be shown how to milk; you have to adjust to it. They could tell you certain little things, like how to work your thumbs and your finger, and you're drawing it down. Once the cow relaxed with you the milk went into the pail. From there, it went into a [machine] that had a special filter, in case it had anything in it; then it went through the cooler. After that, I was assigned to bottle the milk, but some of it went away in big vehicles that came to collect it. The cows were milked twice a day, in the morning and at about 5 o'clock at night. If they were out in the fields, you had to bring them in. That was an experience at the beginning, as well, because they used to run all over the road, and you had to get them all together, as many as 20 cows!

I lived in the hostel, about a mile from the farm, maybe just over a mile. It had two large Nissen huts, wooden chalet-type of things with metal stoves right in the middle that you used to put coke in. There were eight two-tiered bunk beds, and you had two blankets, a sheet and a pillow; and you had a box underneath to put your [clothes] in. You were issued with shoes and tee-shirts, corduroy knee-length trousers and long stockings that you wore to the knee and then turned over, an overcoat, a milking coat, and a hat, of course, with the badge, and your green tie. The pullover I knitted myself. Your underwear you had to supply yourself.

You got up about 6.30am and you had your breakfast, and collected your packed lunch, and you walked to the farm – uphill; downhill coming back, so it wasn't too bad! Some of [the girls] went to market gardens and other farms right the way round the area, and they went about six in a van and they were dropped off at the different farms. You had to collect the cows in the summer because [the farmers] used to let them out in May when the grass was coming on the fields. But in the autumn and winter, they were all let into a big yard, where you had to go and clean up after them; you had to swill all the place out and it was heavy work.

During the summer, it was hay time and I worked on that. We used to go round the edge of the field with a big scythe, the men and me as well, there were three of us. Then they got the horses in for the cutting of the hay – it was all horses; there were no tractors. The hay was mounded, and then I kept turning it over for it to dry, over a few days. That was when I was left on my own. It was gradually formed into big heaps and then they used to bring in the horses with the bogey which was flat, and they used to slide the mound onto it, and that was taken to the farmyard and then put into the barns. They didn't have any sides, and the hay was just heaped in them. We could be working until half past ten at night, because if the weather forecast was telling you it was going to rain, you had to get in the hay. The farmer's wife used to bring us hot scones out of the oven, and gooseberry tart, with big flagons of tea. It was nice sitting in the sunshine; we had about half an hour to eat the scones; and the milk was lovely in the tea. The gooseberry tart was a bit tart, because sugar was rationed. But that treat I'll always remember.

When the corn came, that was stooked like a pack of cards and, later on, when it was dried out it was [packed] with the corn at one end and the stalks at the other, stacked one on top of the other. Then it was time for the harvest, when the threshing machine used to come around, and that was a very busy time. They used to come from other farms to help out. Threshing was a very dirty, dusty job. The corn went through [the thresher] and it went into sacks; and the straw was sort of tied together when it came out. I was up in the loft of this barn, and the men had to fork it up to me, and I had to pack it. That was the straw that was used for the bedding for the cows and horses.

**Miss Kit Knox & friend
planting spuds.**

We used to plant potatoes as well. You had them in a big apron, and I remember the potato-planting was the length of my foot: you put one in and went the length of one foot and then you put in another one. The furrow had been prepared by the farmer or one of the men. The men folk and the horses would drill them up again afterwards. They did the same with turnips. The turnip seeds were planted with this seed implement that used to go round and just drop the seeds in several rows done all together, and then they were furrowed. It was my job to be in the field on my own for the whole day with a nine inch [23cm] hoe. I left one, or maybe two, turnip seeds that had just come through with the first lot of leaves, and knocked the rest out because you didn't want them. When the turnips were ready in November you had to go with your gloves and all your gear on, in the really icy cold, for them to be collected. The turnips were all churned up by another piece of machinery that got them out of the soil. You had a great big knife but it was curved; you used to lift the turnips up and knock the end off, and knock the head off, and then just leave the turnip. They were gathered later on and stored in the farmyard. If it was a rainy day, the farmer would make me go into the shed and sort out the small turnips and potatoes for the animals to eat. I had to put them through a machine and I was a bit afraid of that. It was like a big old-fashioned mangle and it used to chop them all up.

With having to work Saturdays and Sundays – the cows still had to be milked – we all took our turn for having a weekend off. It used to take me three buses to get home and I'd get home at about 4 o'clock on a Saturday afternoon and then I had to leave at 4 o'clock on the Sunday; so I didn't get to see much of my family. I had about every third weekend off, but it used to eat up all your money with the travelling, because you didn't get paid very much (but you got your food). The time we finished in the evening varied; you used to take turns again with finishing. When the clocks changed and it got dark about 4-ish, you milked the cows earlier, so you got away earlier. If you were lucky, you could get a bath when you got back, but there were all the other girls– if they were in before you, then you wouldn't get the hot water, and you'd just have to have a cold wash. If you went to the cinema, you never saw the end of the film because the last bus from Darlington left before the end; the same at Stockton.

When we had our midday break, we used to go back to the farmhouse, which was lovely and warm, and there were these lovely smells. You sat on a separate table from the family and ate your packed lunch from the hostel! Sometimes Mrs Shepherd would offer us some soup. It was always *Workers' Playtime*[8] at half past twelve, and as soon as that finished, we had to get back to work. Packed lunch was always sandwiches with cheese, and what wasn't used up would be fried on both sides, and put in the oven, and we'd have that as supper. That was always after your evening meal though, and if you'd been out to the chippy, you didn't bother with these horrid sandwiches. There were always flagons of cocoa.

Sometimes at the weekend I'd go and pick strawberries at a market garden, but I didn't get paid for it: I just got paid in kind by being able to take strawberries home for my family. And the farmer's wife used to say, 'Cream it off and you can take some cream home'; so it was really nice to get home at about 4 o'clock, for my parents and brothers to have strawberries and cream.

I had an accident on a bike – I fell on it and I hurt my pelvis so I was off for a few weeks, so when I was well again, I was assigned to another farm where they didn't have cows, just poultry and pigs. And that was an experience again because we used to smell when we were doing the mucking out; nobody sat beside you on the bus when you were going back to the hostel! The greatest shock I got was when I had to go into an outhouse once – it was near Christmas – and there were the geese hanging up, slit throats and dripping; the farmer hadn't forewarned me. It was the same when they stunned a pig as well. They scrubbed it with boiling water and then it was slaughtered but I don't know what happened after that. I do remember the woman mixing the blood for the black pudding and I just didn't like that very much. So the pig was cut up, then salted and hung up for bacon. Well, I got this nice box for Christmas and when I opened it, it was the pig's tail, with a big blue bow on – that's what I got for my Christmas present! So that was rather a shock; I think it's the only part of the pig you can't eat, apart from its eyes.

At Middleton St George there was the Canadian Air Force and we used to hear the bombers when they were going out and when they were coming back. It was a low sound going out, because they were heavy with bombs, and then you were listening for them coming back and it was a different sound. We could hear the sirens going off towards Teesside and the searchlights were always going. We used to go outside and watch, and we could see them in the sky. We could hear the guns firing as well.

I enjoyed it all, though. You didn't really realise there was a war on. It was only afterwards, and as I got older, that I realised what it was all about.

The Timber Corps

Also known as 'Lumber Jills', these women were part of the WLA, but they were assigned to work in the forests, sawmills and other timber-related places.

Miss Kathleen High

Kathleen High was only 16 when she became a Lumber Jill in her native Cumbria. Here, she gives a vivid account of her work in the forests near her home.

I was in [the Timber Corps] from the beginning, and I was in for seven years. When war broke out, I was doing domestic work in Appleby; I was 16 on 9 September [1939], and I should've been 17 to join the Land Army, but I joined and they left it at that! We were clothed: the Land Army dungarees and the breeches, so it did save our own clothes.

I cycled [to work] and then a lorry used to pick us up in the Appleby area and take us to where we were going. I used to set off from home at about 7 o'clock every morning, and we picked the wagon up at about half seven. We finished roughly about 5 o'clock and it'd be nearly six by the time I got home. I used to go to a lot of the smaller woods because they used to send me around. When I first went to Flakebridge forest, the wood fellas sawed the trees down and they were put in rows. It was more or less all pine. I used to measure them individually, with a long tape measure, and I sawed them with a small bushman's saw. It was a one-handled saw and I used it on my own.

The logs were for pit props for the mines, and also telegraph poles. You had to peel the trees, and it was very hard work. It was better if the sap was running. If you didn't peel them before the sap [stopped]

running and they were dried, they weren't so easy to do. That was for the telegraph poles. We peeled them with a scraper on a handle, and you were pushing it to scrape them. Then it got to the saw benches, where there were two men cutting for the pit props. I stacked them after that. They were different sizes: four feet, five feet, six feet [1.2m,

1.5m, 1.8m]; and the diameter was the girth of about six or seven inches [15-17cm]. They were heavy to lift but I used to lift them if it wasn't a huge great one.

I eventually went to a bigger forest on the outskirts of Appleby, and they were huge trees. They had a terrible big girth and I used to have to get somebody to help me put the tape measure through, to get the girth. We had a big saw mill in there and I went into the saw mill for a while. Some of them had a girth of 20 inches [50cm], maybe more. We knew how old a tree was when it was down because we started in the middle and counted the rings all the way out. We used to burn the brushwood as well, to get shot of all the rubbish. You used to have it in the sides, at a distance, with the trees in the middle. Then you had to get the trees out, which were snigged [dragged] by horses with chains. That was at first; then it was with tractors. The logs were pulled out to a certain place to stack them and lorries used to come and collect them.

Sometimes I would help the fellas to saw the tree down, not very often, but I loved to do that. The men used to gob it on the front, very near the ground, and I went in the back when the tree fell over. Then the branches were all to trim with an axe, though the men did that; I never did. Then we measured them and girthed them. Those trees weren't stripped – they went into the saw mill, where they used to saw them into planks.

In summer, we used to have to cope with ant heaps. They used to grow about four feet high and they were always busy. I was frightened stiff of them because if I got bitten, I used to come up in lumps.

I was always very hungry, and I think my mother had an awful time to feed us. When I got home at night, I could've eaten two dinners many a time! It being wartime, you only got so much food. They didn't provide us with food; you had your own lunch to take. Sometimes we'd take a meat sandwich or cheese, an odd piece of cake, maybe a bit of fruit. We used to have an open fire and put a little kettle on. We used to club together and get tea, and then make our own. In some of the places they had little sheds that you could go into if it was wet. It varied a bit – you'd have maybe half an hour to an hour. It would depend on what you were doing. Sometimes the wood fellas liked to get on after about half an hour – some of them were on piece work, you see.

We had a holiday in summer, but we wouldn't be all off together, and we had three weeks, or maybe a month towards the end of the war. I worked mostly Monday to Friday, but sometimes I worked at the weekend. It varied: if there was something to catch up on, or if they wanted something doing, and we'd get paid [extra] for what we did. When I first started it was £2.50 a week; my dad was working on the Council and I was making two or three shillings a week more than he was and he didn't like that very much! We laughed about it afterwards. For a toilet they had a little hut, and [the toilet] was dug into the ground, and it was shared, men and women – when you're out in the wilds, that's it, isn't it!

Mostly we were careful and there weren't many accidents, but there was one person who lost an arm when he was on the saw bench; and there was one man whose leg was run over by the tractor because the ground was soft.

On our time off we used to cycle on a Saturday to the pictures down in Appleby; and there was the odd dance, about once a month. The locals would go to them, but we also had the army on Brackenber Moor – in the summertime they used to tent there – and there was the army camp at Warcop, and they'd come to the dances if they were allowed out. We were once invited up to theirs when there was a Henry Hall[9] show. We went to the camp and listened to the band; it was lovely. They invited the local people as well – it wasn't just the Land Army. Warcop was a training camp and they came from everywhere, even young cadets in the summer season for an odd week. Occasionally we'd go to Penrith to the pictures – we'd go on the bus, but we didn't go regularly. It was all marvellous really. It was hard work, but it was a wonderful life.

The Voluntary Aid Detachment (VAD)

The Voluntary Aid Detachment was created in 1909 with the help of the Red Cross and Order of St John, and was a voluntary organisation. It provided auxiliary nursing services, mainly in hospitals, in both Britain and other parts of the Empire.

By the end of 1914, there were 74,000 VADs, of which two thirds were women and girls. Nurses were in short supply when the First World War broke out, so VADs supplemented the work of registered nurses. They were generally looked down on by the trained and qualified nursing staff, but they nevertheless provided a vital support to the war effort.

The main responsibilities of a VAD were those of a nursing orderly in hospitals. She carried out menial but essential jobs such as sweeping, dusting and cleaning, scrubbing floors, dealing with bedpans, and giving bed baths to or washing patients. They were not used in military hospitals, except as ward and pantry maids, but they were employed in Red Cross convalescent and rest homes, canteens, and on troop trains. Some VADs acted as letter writers for soldiers who were either too ill or too illiterate to write.

Before 1915, the authorities would not allow VADs at the front-line, but this rule was later relaxed and volunteer VADs over the age of 23 and with more than three months' experience, were allowed to go. They served on the Western Front, in Mesopotamia and Gallipoli, and also on the Eastern Front.

The role of VADs did not fundamentally change between the wars, but VADs in the Second World War were given more medical training. They were still not fully qualified nurses, however. They worked on hospital ships, in convalescent hospitals, and on the home front.

Miss EL, Voluntary Aid Detachment

Miss EL had always wanted to be a nurse but wasn't able to fulfil her ambition because she was needed to help her brother run the family business. She was able to do some nursing work during her spare time, as she became a member of the Red Cross.

When the war broke out, she registered for war work but didn't express a preference, as she thought her call-up would be deferred. However, she was called up in 1942, being placed 'where the needs were greatest', with the ATS. So she went to see her Red Cross commandant who tore up the papers and sent her for a medical.

> And the next Wednesday I went to Howick Hall which was a Red Cross auxiliary hospital near Craster on the Northumberland coast. It was a convalescent home. We had ENSA concerts sometimes because Howick was out of Alnwick and there wasn't much for the patients to do. We had a doctor who was, I think, Russian, and he used to come and play the piano; and we had dances at Howick.
>
> [But] I wanted to get on and be in some action, you see, so after ten months, I went to see Lady Grey who lived there (she'd given

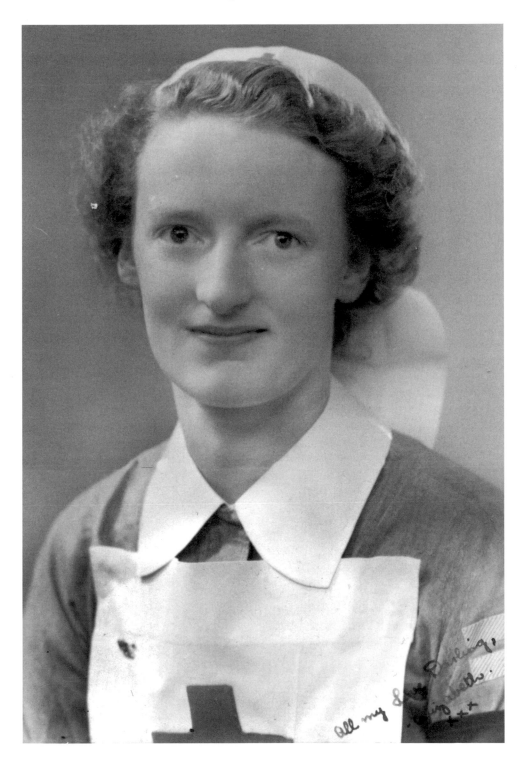

up her home to the hospital and was living in the west wing), and said to her I would like a move and I wanted to go to the Navy. She said the Red Cross County Director was coming the next week and she would see what [could be done]. And so, I got into the Navy!

I went to Plymouth. It was a long way from home and it took me 12 hours to get there, because there were no direct trains and I had to go via London. When we got [to Plymouth], after midnight and in the blackout, there were sailors there with a truck to take us from the station – there were two of us. We got our meal, and then when we went upstairs. It wasn't very nice: the windows wouldn't shut and the doors wouldn't shut – it had all been bombed;

We went to the hospital the next morning by transport as it was half an hour away, and the commander said, 'Now don't press these nurses too hard today. They've had a long journey and they must be very tired'.

The windows [of the hospital] were all bricked up – there was no daylight. Downstairs was all empty for air raid casualties and all the hospital was upstairs. I was on the medical ward, and it was seriously ill people we were looking after there. They were mostly the result of injuries and accidents; [they were] troops from the hospital ships coming in. As soon as they were convalescent, they were evacuated to leave space for the next ones coming in.

We worked a 12-hour day one day, and the next day we had half a day off. Sometimes at a weekend, we could get somebody to work for us on a Saturday morning, and we got two days off together, and we were able to get home. But then, you'd have to have two 12-hour days together the next week. So we were tired and worn out. It was hard work – these 12-hour days meant you were absolutely jiggered at the end. And we had to wash up the dishes and lay the breakfast before we went upstairs; then there were queues for the toilet, queues for the bath; queues for everything – facilities were bad! Plymouth was so badly bombed and the nurses' Mess had all been flattened, so they took all these houses way outside and round about, and that's how we were housed. They were empty houses where people had fled away from all the bombing.

Plymouth was nearly flattened[10] so there was no place to go. You got perhaps three hours off in the middle of the day but there wasn't anywhere to go. There was just the Plymouth Hoe and dancing, but that was all – there wasn't any recreation at all. I can't tell you how awful it was. However we stood that for several weeks, and then one day Matron sent for us and said, 'I'm sending you two girls nearer home – you're going to Liverpool,' and I was there till I was demobbed.

We were not expected to leave the hospital until we'd got the [casualties] all settled down – it was sometimes past midnight before we got them settled. You'd see [a hospital ship] sailing past and you knew you were in for a late night! The troops were all brought into the corridors and that's when we got them. They were all looked after [on the hospital ship, and had had some medical attention]. When we got them, the condition they were in varied – some had metal through their innards, some were seriously ill, some were put in plaster casts. The ones with shrapnel didn't have operations on the ship because they were coming from war zones, so they had operations in [the Liverpool] hospital, and I assisted with those. My first operation was a nasal operation, and I was backing for the door when I saw all the blood running! However, I got used to that. Eventually my last job lasted quite a long time. I worked for an ear, nose and throat specialist. We got tonsillectomies by the dozen, nose operations, and mastoids we did in those days.

We lived in a nurses' home in Waterloo, which was three or four miles away from the hospital. It was a lovely big house taken over. We had a huge room; seven of us were in there; seven beds, seven chests of drawers, seven lockers. Every day we got to the hospital by transport – a bus in the morning and a lorry with the Wrens when it was half shift.

If anybody was on the danger list, the relatives had free transport to come and visit; but sometimes nobody ever came.

We had a lot of fun when we were off duty. We worked hard and played hard. When we were off duty, we used to bathe at Freshfield. We went for fortune telling; we had parties; we went to Southport and to Chester, and they were full of American soldiers. We got a lift from them through the Mersey Tunnel, and the same coming back, but we never did that unless there was a few of us! One of the girls had an American boyfriend, and she used to bring in all sorts of lovely things – food and sweets, and chocolate – and she shared these things; she gave me loads of things.

When we were on duty, we were looking after the patients' welfare. The patients were all service people, and all men – we had

VAD EL in outdoor uniform.

no women. We were doing everything: changing beds, getting [the patients] washed and bathed; then there was the medicine round, the doctor's round, pulse and respirations to take; do the dressings, set the trolleys. There were no trained nurses – just the Sister and the VADs. Matron just came about once a week, and she was always in her coat and hat, never working – the Sisters were doing all that!

The Sisters had to do split shifts as well, and for one afternoon, they had to do two wards. The doctor was there a lot. He had his outpatients to see, and then he had the ward to look after. We had a special doctor for each ward. Sometimes they were there at 7 o'clock in the morning before we went on duty. They were regular navy [doctors] and would be there all the time until they were moved, and then they were off.

When D–Day was building up, we lost all the men – they were scattered and away into the war, and we were left with just an odd man or two. Leave was all stopped. The ships were building up in Liverpool and we knew something was going on. Then all the casualties kept coming in, and as soon as they'd picked up a bit, they were evacuated to convalescent homes, and you got another lot. There was great activity but we coped with it all. It was when the hospital ships came in there was more demand and we were not allowed off duty until they'd all been cleared away.

It was a good war. We had a lot of fun.

Queen Alexandra's Imperial Military Nursing Service (QAIMNS)

The Queen Alexandra's Imperial Military Nursing Service (QAIMNS) was founded in 1902, established by Royal Warrant, and named after Queen Alexandra, the wife of Edward VII, and who became its President. It was the nursing branch of the British Army and part of the Army Medical Services, and comprised qualified nurses.

By the outbreak of war in 1914, there were only 297 regular members of the QAIMNS, mainly because of its strict acceptance rules. Women had to be unmarried, over 25 years of age, and of a high social status. Because of the enormous casualty rates during the Great War, these restrictions had to be removed. Then, more than 10,000 qualified nurses joined the QAIMNS Reserve, which for the first time included married women and those of a lower social class. By the end of 1914, there were over 2,200 regular and reserve QAs and when the war ended, there were more than 10,400 trained nurses in the service. The QAs tended to the wounded in field hospitals, aboard ambulance trains, hospital ships and hospital barges and in casualty clearing stations.

During the Second World War, each nurse had officer status, but no actual commission status; therefore, they were not subject to military discipline. However, in 1941, emergency commissions and rank structure were formulated to bring the QAs into line with the rest of the British Army. QAs were then able to be promoted.

During the war, recruitment for army nurses was so successful that in 1943, a restriction was put into place stating that only newly-qualified nurses could enlist. This meant that the more experienced nurses stayed in Britain to care for the casualties of air raids and to nurse evacuated soldiers back to health.

Nursing Sister ES (QAIMNS)

Nursing Sister ES went from practising midwifery and general nursing in a rural area of England to caring for wartime patients in India – a huge difference. Her experiences were the stuff that films are made of – being torpedoed out of the water, undergoing an aerial attack by enemy aircraft, and becoming caught up in an armed mutiny. Surviving all these events unscathed, she experienced several years in India working with British and West African troops and also Indian patients, all of which she remembers with affection and, even now, a sense of amazement.

> I was District Nurse Midwife; there was a war on, and I wanted to do my bit – I wanted to be with the services. I knew about the Queen Alexandra's, of course. We weren't commissioned officers in those days; we were all trained nurses and not subject to military discipline. I applied to join in 1942 but, because I was also a practising midwife, I wasn't accepted then. I applied again at the end of 1942, and was accepted; and I had to be released by the county I was working for. They released me, but six months after that I wouldn't have been able to [join the QAIMNS]. They were so short of midwives in the country by then, because people were all joining up, that I wouldn't have been accepted, so I was rather lucky that way.
>
> I actually went into the army in March 1943 and I went to York Military Hospital. I had a very difficult time – it was a very different life from civilian life. Conditions were sparse and basic in the wards, but the treatment was excellent. We were very near a lot of airfields and we had a lot of air crash casualties coming back. We had very primitive conditions in those days for casualties. We had one ward where we received all the casualties on stretchers which were laid on trestles all down one side. We had beds on the other side and as

the [patients] were checked over they were transferred. We had blankets over the trestles to the floor and primus stoves underneath for heat – it was field conditions, really. I was at York for only a matter of weeks, and I did most of my work on night duty. I then went up to Scotland, and was then transferred to the Turnberry Hotel [Ayrshire] which we took over as a military hospital. From there, I eventually went down to London, where we mobilised and I went out to India, in October 1943.

We sailed from Liverpool on a troopship called the *Marnix St Aldegonde*, which was a commandeered Dutch merchant vessel. The crew were mainly Lascars from the Dutch East Indies[11], except the officers, who were British. It was rather strange because we set sail, and the next morning we were back where we started from! I think there must have been a message that we weren't allowed to go for some reason, but we set sail again 24 hours later. We went down to the English Channel, through the Straits of Gibraltar and, on 6 November, we were torpedoed. We were sailing along in convoy; I think ours was the last troopship in the convoy. It was a very busy ship and we had meals in two servings. We were in the first serving and we went down to the dining room for dinner at half-past six, and we had just sat down when the alarm bells on the ship went. Everyone just shot up because we felt the movement; we felt the torpedo hit us; we felt the ship jerk.

Of course, we'd all been rehearsed in drill and we knew exactly what we had to do, which was to return to our cabins. The ship was listing heavily and on the next signal we had to go to our lifeboat stations. We went in formation along the gangways to a lifeboat station on deck A, but our lifeboat had been shattered, so we were transferred to the deck below. The ship was listing very heavily and all the sailors were lined up – it was quite incredible, really.

We were put into a lifeboat and lowered into the sea. We didn't quite know what was happening but we heard afterwards that the people on the top above us were worried whether the lifeboat would tip over. But we landed in the sea all right, and moved away. The lifeboat was absolutely crowded, and we couldn't use oars at all. We had a young sailor who'd had his appendix out that morning and he was lying on the side of the lifeboat.

So there we were in the sea: it was a November night and it was very wet, and there was a big swell on. We sat there and we moved off away from the ship, and we saw our ship go down, actually. There was no fire. We saw it tip and then go down the following morning in daylight. We just floated round in the sea and we'd all been very violently sick; but we had tin hats, of course, which came in very useful, as you can imagine! We sat in rows, and I never thought I was in any particular danger – it was amazing, really. We chatted to each other and there was no panic; there was nothing; it was just quiet, everyone was quiet. Eventually, we heard the chug of a motor boat, and they were the search vessels coming out, looking for the lifeboats. We saw a light approaching and they came [towards us]. The petrol fumes were dreadful – I remember that because we were all feeling weak and the petrol fumes were dreadful. The search vessel towed us to a destroyer – the *HMS Coomb* – and we were picked up by that. We had to get onto the destroyer one by one on the crest of a wave, when the lifeboat was at its highest, onto a rope ladder, and up onto the deck. I had no head for heights, but it's amazing what you can do when you have to – you just do it! The destroyer picked up 400 – 500 people from the Med that night. We never knew whether there was any loss of life because we weren't

Nursing Sister ES, (QAIMNS) in Algiers November 1943, after being torpedoed in the Mediterranean Sea.

allowed to ask any questions. There was a war on; you weren't allowed to tell anyone; even writing home, you couldn't say what had happened; you weren't allowed to discuss it, even. All letters were censored and so we never really knew what happened.[12]

So we were now on the destroyer. As you can imagine, there were many of us on board, but they were absolutely wonderful. They did provide some soup, but there were so many of us, they couldn't provide meals. They made for the nearest port which, in those days, was Philippeville in Algiers. We were landed there at about half-past ten at night; that would be on 7 November. There had been quite a number of QAs on board, because we were sailing out to Burma with a hospital. We'd had all the equipment and a full staff; and we lost everything. There was a military hospital in the area – the 67th General – and we were taken there in trucks. We joined up with our colleagues because they'd been in different lifeboats. We were all checked in, and we were all there. No one had been lost which was rather lovely.

We didn't have anyone in charge of us, but we had a senior officer who was going out to be Matron in Charge in the Far East. She checked us all in and more or less took over. We were put up under canvas. We didn't have anything except what we stood up in, but we were all alright. We were all given something from the Red Cross: bags with toilet things, and a 50-tin of cigarettes, which was the thing to do, whether you smoked or not, (it's amazing when you think about it today!). We didn't have any clothes – I was in a ward dress when we were torpedoed. There was an officers' shop in Philippeville, but there was really nothing there for women, so we just had to manage with what we could get. We got officers' kit and we got men's battledress, army boots or officers' shoes.

We were there for about a month and then we sailed off through the Mediterranean, and we were attacked again at night, from the air, just off Alexandria. It was an aerial attack, German planes that had come over from Italy, I think. Every gun on the ship was in use and the noise was terrific. We all went to our cabins and just stayed there and listened to everything. Eventually things quietened down and we were still sailing. We had a wonderful captain. At 11 o'clock at night, he broadcast over the Tannoy, 'I want you all to rest. Get onto your bunks, fully dressed, wearing your lifejackets'. He was so good – he kept us informed of what was happening. So that was that, and the journey proceeded uneventfully. We went through the Suez Canal and we stopped off at Port Tufic. We went ashore to a transit camp, again under canvas on the sand, to try and get some equipment. We were issued with some First World War dresses which had long sleeves with tapes at the cuffs, white wool gloves, and a sewing kit so we could shorten the sleeves and turn them up. We were there for two or three days and then we rejoined the ship, and we sailed across to Bombay without any further problems. We arrived on about 22 or 23 December – quite a long journey out – and from there we were dispersed all over India. Four of us went to Poona (Pune) to the military hospital, and then we went to Meerut which was about 60 miles from Delhi. Then I went to an RAF hospital in Chakrata up in the Himalayan foothills, before being posted to Aundh [north-west of Poona/ Pune], to the West African military hospital.

There I had great experiences with the West African troops – they were lovely; they were so jolly. They spoke pidgin English and so of course, we tried to speak pidgin English too. Every now and then we would get ambulances arriving with other troops who were being sent back from Burma, and all the patients who were up used to go and look for their brothers, as they said, and it was chaos! We were given a list of those who were seriously ill, and we went to the ambulances and saw they were transferred to beds straight away. Some of them had battle injuries, illnesses or wounds, jungle sores, fractures, tropical illnesses, everything. But all the others just sorted themselves out; it was amazing, really. On New Year's Eve 1944, I went on ambulance duty, on an ambulance train, right across to Madras, to pick up Africans coming out of the jungle, those who'd been injured. That was very interesting. It was a long trip, a tremendous journey on the train, right across India. When we got there, we picked up Africans from ambulances. Unfortunately, the air conditioning had failed, so it was very hot. There were bunk beds in the carriages and as the troops came on board, they were frightened to go up on the bunk beds: 'I no go for up'. They'd never seen anything like that before – they were primitive, really, out of the jungle, you see. They went out to Burma to chop trees down in the jungle; that's what their job was. They'd never seen an ambulance train in their lives; some of them had never even seen a train. But eventually we persuaded them to go up. They were like children and we had bags of sweeties for them, and things like that. Once they'd got up a height, they thought it was marvellous and they wouldn't come down! They thought it was great being up there, and we had a lot of fun with them. Those who were least injured we put on the top bunks and the more seriously injured we had on the lower bunks. We took them back to Aundh, to the base hospital.

Eventually, I was posted from there to another West African unit up in Bengal, just on the Burma border. I was there for only about two months when we had an armed mutiny. That's a long story. It was a tented hospital, and the African patients were lovely. We weren't allowed to do any night duties – the Africans had come from West Africa, I don't think they knew where they'd been, but there were no women there – so we weren't allowed to be alone with them. There were only 12 of us, and we weren't allowed to be outside of our compound without escort. Two of our nursing sisters decided to have a walk one night outside the compound and they were attacked by one of the Africans. They weren't hurt – I don't know what exactly happened; I never found that out – but they weren't hurt. The African who'd attacked them was sent for trial, and some of the more educated Africans, those who'd been mission-educated, decided that if this boy was found guilty, they would attack us, they would attack the staff. It's a long story but he was found guilty. I was on duty, as we all were, and the CO sent the medical officers round to remove us all from our duties. We all went back to our huts which were bashas made of straw; we each had one of these. We were scared while it was going on. One of our medical officers got out and went for help from the Indian Rajput Rifle regiment, which was the nearest rifle regiment to us. The CO would not leave his tent and duty – his two staff sergeants begged him to leave his tent, but he would not; and one of the West Africans shot him, just sitting behind his desk. He was a lovely chap; he was very fond of the African troops. The Indian Rajput Rifles then took control, but by this time all 12 of us were together in one little basha. We thought if we were going to be attacked at least we'd be together. Eventually, we were all taken out under armed guard to some place where we were able to stay for a few days. Then we were dispersed again and I ended up near Calcutta where I stayed until October 1946. That was quite an interesting experience. I was in charge of a families' hospital in Calcutta, where we had mainly midwifery, with the troops' wives.

Most hospitals [I worked in] had an Indian section and a British section, but we also staffed the Indian hospitals. We had medical wards, surgical, everything. The patients always came from the units serving in India, from the Indian army and the British army. Usually the hospitals were Nissen-type huts, and the Indian hospitals were quite incredible. Life was cheap in India. Sometimes we had patients who were scheduled as seriously ill, and we'd go round at night and find they'd gone to the local bazaar; or we'd find their goats sleeping under the bed – this was normal; you got used to this sort of thing. We worked long hours, in the heat. We normally started work at half-past seven until one o'clock – we did tropical hours – and the next day we'd work from one till eight. In our time off, we largely entertained ourselves. Occasionally we had an ENSA concert; and we had a lot of Mess parties. In June '44 we had a party to celebrate D-Day, and we had a so-called dance, but it was just our Mess and the officers' Mess, really, and they put a tarpaulin on the ground so that we could dance. I can't remember where the music came from, probably somebody's gramophone. I remember trying to dance and there were these big flies, sticky things, and they were flying around and catching you – dreadful really. We had lots of fun amongst ourselves. The comradeship was wonderful – that's the one thing I think I missed the most when I first came home. Apart from a short period in Darjeeling, I spent my last year at the Military Hospital in Calcutta.

The National Fire Service (NFS)

The National Fire Service was formed in August 1941, when the local authority fire brigades in England, Scotland and Wales were combined. Its remit was to deal more effectively with the fires started by air raids, and its members were both full- and part-time, and male and female, although the women were mostly employed in an administrative capacity. It was one of the services that some conscientious objectors joined, as it was non-combative, but its work was crucial to the war effort, and the country's survival. Often, the men were part-time because their 'day job' was a reserved occupation. Workers were exempt from call-up if they were in farming or agriculture, railways and docks, mining, teaching and medicine. Engineering was the industry with the highest number of exemptions.

Mrs VP, National Fire Service

In 1942, at the age of 21, Mrs VP opted to join the NFS after she failed her medical for the armed services. She had been a civil servant working in London for the Ministry of Health, which was evacuated to Blackpool to escape the Blitz, Mrs VP being part of the exodus.

> We were all working in various hotels at the beginning of the war. There was very little going on at the beginning; it was very quiet. When we went to Blackpool, we had air raid sirens going but we had no raids at all – all the raids were going to Liverpool and Manchester. If the air raid sirens went off, everybody went about their business as usual!

As a civil servant, she was already working for the government, but she was required by law to do extra 'war work'.

> I had the choice of either Queen Alexandra's Nursing or the National Fire Service. I was too squeamish and I jokingly said I would kill more than I cured if I was in the nurses, so I chose the Fire Service. There were two girls on [duty] each night and we only had to go three nights a week, every other night, but there was nothing going on at all. We went to a hall, and it was only a sub-station, a part-time station. We didn't open until 7 o'clock at night and we used to go home at 11.00 pm. We had one fire engine and there was just one group of men who were firemen, and they were part-timers as well, because they were all tradesmen. We didn't receive any training at all, so I don't know what we'd have done if anything had happened! Whether the men did, I don't know, but we didn't. They did once jokingly say to another girl and me, 'Do you want to take the fire engine to pieces?' but we said, 'No – you might not get it back!' I was there until 1943 and we never had a call-out.

At home in London, Mrs VP's mother became very ill, needing 24-hour care, so she had to leave Blackpool and return to help the family with her mother's nursing. Still working as a civil servant, she was transferred to the Ministry of Agriculture, which had returned to London from its previous evacuation to Bournemouth. Because she was in the NFS, Mrs

VP still had to do war work and so she joined the fire service nearest to her home.

We had eight big fire stations where I lived and that's where I had to report [for duty]. Duty was only two nights a week, but I had to be there at 7 o'clock – you daren't be a minute late; it was very, very [strict] – and you were on all night, until 7 o'clock the next day. There were a lot of us, and we did shifts – 7.00pm to 11.00pm, 11.00pm to 3.00am and 3.00am to 7.00am, and it was a rota, so one time you were on 7.00pm to 11.00pm, the next time on 11.00pm to 3.00am and so on. The girls did mainly telephone work on the switchboards, taking messages and giving messages, about where fire engines were needed, about fire bombs especially at one time, or you got messages coming through to the [Chief Officer] of the station. I'd never seen a switchboard before and they never told you anything; they just said, 'There it is'. The very first message I took, I wanted the senior man of the fire station and I knew I had to put the plug in. Well, I obviously did a wrong thing because he came flying down and – I wasn't used to bad language – he, you know . . . By all accounts, what I had done meant that the noise would have gone into his ear and it really would have given him [pain]. Later he came back and said, 'I'm sorry. I shouldn't have said what I said to you'. But I learnt then that you don't put the plug in that one!

Occasionally you were thrown into what was called a mobile [shift], and so you didn't do any duty at all in the station itself, but you could go up into the women's room, which was right at the top of the building, a big building it was, and there were bunk beds so you could sleep if you wished. When the raids started, if you were mobile, you were taken to another place and if I was on mobile, usually I went to a school where there was a switchboard and you had to take all the [phone] messages. It wasn't particularly good if there were bombs or shrapnel coming down! But we had our steel helmets and our gas masks; you never went anywhere without your gas mask and your steel helmet.

We had a uniform; it was navy blue with red [trim]. We had a jacket and slacks, and we also had a skirt, but mainly we wore the slacks. We had a little cap like a Glengarry which you could bring the [sides] down and button up, but mine never came open, I'm afraid! I wish I'd kept my cap, really, but I just parted with it …

While still in Blackpool, Mrs VP had to return home to London to attend a family funeral in September 1940.

> The Blitz was very, very bad. None of our houses had big gardens and there were big air raid shelters in the road. They were built of brick and had an opening [for you] to get in, and they were quite high. The floor was made of cement. They were in two halves: you could go through this opening and you went either that side or [the other] side. It was horrible inside; it smelt earthy to me. There wasn't a lot of electric, and there was just a little bit of lighting to see where you were. You couldn't read and there was nothing you could do. People used to just sit and chat, and then you'd lie down and go to sleep. Every night from about half past five on, we used to take our bedding out, and drinks and so forth, and the next morning, you'd collect your bedding [and leave]. I hated it and in fact I rebelled and I said to my father, 'I'm not going in there'. We had a neighbour just along the road who refused to go in . . . so as soon as the air raid started, I used to go there. A lot of people would go to the railway stations and sleep on the platforms. We never had windows [in our house] – they were blown out so many times. They would come and put new ones in for you, and then they'd be blown out again!
>
> The doodlebugs had a peculiar sound. You could hear it coming and once it stopped, you knew you were safe because it had gone by you. The V2s just came and you either lived or you didn't. It was a big bomb and you had no warning of it; it was a jet propelled idea, it didn't come in aeroplanes.
>
> We got [air raids] at all times. I was at work in Baker Street and there was only my boss and me, all the rest had gone to lunch. I happened to look out of the window and I said, 'Oh, there's a funny aeroplane coming over. Look at that'. He said, 'That's not an aeroplane, that's a doodlebug – get under the desk!' I was most intrigued. Of course, you could tell a German aeroplane because the engine had a different sound. You began to learn the [difference between] German planes and the British ones.
>
> At that particular time [1940] there was a raid all night long, and you never knew – sometimes it was near you. This is what I found [upsetting] when I was on duty when the raids were on, because I wasn't sure what was happening at home. I lived in Holloway, and

you'd get messages coming through, 'It's in Holloway at the moment' and you could tell by the noise.

It got really busy. A lot of the messages were to send engines out, and I had to give them to the senior [officer] who then gave the orders. You were very busy receiving messages, and you also had to send messages to other sub-stations that maybe were nearer [the fire]. What angered the firemen was false alarms. You got people making false alarms and [the firemen] would go. Sometimes they'd been on a proper alarm and had just come back tired, and had had a hectic time, then they'd get another call and get there to find there's nothing there at all. They would come back and they were absolutely furious.

Different things happened during the war, but we had a lot of fun.

The Navy, Army & Air Force Institutes (NAAFI)

The Navy, Army and Air Force Institutes (NAAFI) was created in 1921 by the government, to run recreational establishments for the British armed forces, and to sell goods to servicemen and their families. It runs clubs, bars, shops, supermarkets, launderettes, restaurants, cafés and other facilities on most British military bases and also canteens on board Royal Navy ships. The facilities are for junior ranks only, with commissioned officers being expected to use their own Messes.

In 1915, the predecessor of the NAAFI was the Expeditionary Force Canteen, which was established to support the troops on active service abroad. In 1918, the Navy and Army Canteen Board was set up to fulfil the same function at home. These two organisations were then combined in 1921, to form the NAAFI. Its greatest contribution was during the Second World War when, by 1944 it ran 7000 canteens and had 96,000 personnel (from fewer than 600 canteens and 4,000 personnel in 1939). It was also responsible for the Entertainments National Service Association (ENSA), the forces entertainment organisation.

Miss Marjorie Tyson, Navy, Army & Air Force Institutes

Marjorie Tyson started in the NAAFI in 1941, at Walney Aerodrome before moving to the lighthouse off Walney, near Barrow in Furness, Cumbria. Towards the end of the war, she volunteered to go to Belgium,

and found herself there in May 1945, witnessing the aftermath of six years of war, and the German occupation. She finally came home in 1947.

There were only four of us there: the cook, two assistants and the manageress. It was way out, and they allowed us a taxi on a Wednesday to take the money to the bank, otherwise you had to get a lift from the postman or whoever, to get back into Barrow. I was there for nine months and then I went to Haverigg Camp at Millom [Cumbria] and I was there for two years. It was an air force training camp and I quite enjoyed my time there. There were a lot of accidents, and looking out of our window, we'd see the flag at half-mast a lot of the time.

We were up early in the morning to get the floors all scrubbed and ready before dinner. Sometimes we'd have to go out on what was called the Battle Wagon. It was a mobile [unit] where you put a hatch down and served the ones who couldn't get into the canteen, because they were out on the airfield. A tractor used to come and take you, and if that tractor was wanted before you were due to go back, they used to unhook it and leave you there. One time I got into trouble because I stopped up there for two hours. But it meant me walking across the airfield to get back. The manageress said I should've got out, walked and brought my till with me!

They used to make what they called sinker cake, like rock cake. It was pastry and any cakes, or anything that was left, mixed with a bit of spice and then put in the pastry. It was cooked and cut into big squares. It was served warm and it was a filling piece of cake, about thruppence [1.25p] a piece. It used to go well and we had to work it so that when one lot missed out on it, they'd get it next time round.

Marjorie Tyson and friend were told to 'bugger off – this is our patch' by prostitutes when they went to collect this picture from the photographer.

Marjorie Tyson & colleagues at Nutfield Priory, Redhill, before their embarkation for Brussels.

My friend and I had our photograph taken together, and we went back to the studio a few days later to collect the pictures. But he was closed so we stood in the doorway waiting for him to open, and these two women came up to us, and said, 'Bugger off – this is our pitch'. Well, that gave us a good laugh.

From Millom, I put my name down to go [abroad]. We had to go to Redhill [Surrey] and it was one of these big houses with a lake out at the front, and long passages inside [Nutfield Priory]. We were there for VE Day [8 May, 1945] and we were all out that night. We went round the pubs, and there was singing and dancing in the streets. The atmosphere was really good. The pubs were open more or less all day, and there was something going on all day.

We left for Belgium the following week. There were quite a lot of us, and I made friends with one group, so when it came to going to Belgium, I changed from working in the canteen to the warehouse. We went to Ostend and we were there for about a month while they sorted things out for us.

Then we went to Brussels and while we were there, we had about four different billets. We were in one, then they moved us to a chateau, which was quite nice; then they moved us to a small hotel and then they moved us to what was the Palais du Centenaire[13] which was the big exhibition building, and we had the [NAAFI] warehouse there, and we had part of it as living quarters. The army used to come in with their invents [requirements] for what they wanted for their 'tuck shop', and we had to work out what they were allowed to have that week. Whisky was for the officers, and depending on how many officers were in was how many we were allowed to put on the bill. We used to do [several] copies of that: we used to keep one; one used to go into the warehouse for them to put it up, ready; another one they would take, to pay and have it stamped.

When we were in a different billet from the Centenaire, an army truck used to pick us up, and take us to the warehouse. Then we were moved, so we were there, and we started at 8 o'clock in the morning and finished round about teatime.

Quite a few Belgian people worked with us, and if you saw a cross on a corner, with flowers on it, they would tell you [what had happened]. One woman was telling us that she was on a tram and she had her little girl with her. The Germans got on and counted; as it happened, it just missed her. The Germans took them out and shot them.

In Ostend, we kept seeing furniture that had been thrown out of windows. That was where some of the women had gone with the

The Palais du Centenaire, Brussels, where Marjorie Tyson worked and was billeted.

Germans and they'd had their heads shaved[14] – we saw quite a few of them – and all their furniture was just chucked out of their house.

We saw quite a lot of Jewish [troops] who were in the Belgian army. Most of them got on all right, but say you were in a bar or something, and some of them came in, our [troops] were a bit 'off' with them. If they saw you talking to them, they would tell you off.

If you wanted to go down onto the shore, you had to go out of town, because it was fenced off, and all the streets leading down to the shore were barricaded off. So you had to go to Zeebrugge if you wanted to go in the sea. From Brussels we used to go off to different places on a Sunday. We were allowed to use the NAAFI lorry as long as we paid for the petrol, and we once went to the borders of France and Belgium. We'd have a look around before going back. In Brussels there was quite a bit of destruction. Where houses or buildings had been was just clear ground and the rubble had been cleared away.

In the Brussels NAAFI we had Canadians, Americans and our own troops coming through, mostly army, and all different regiments. The civilians were managing all right. Some of the shops around where we were billeted had stuff that we were having a job to get at home, like boxes of cornflakes and things like that. They seemed as if they'd got plenty. The ones who worked with us often used to have a slab of dark chocolate and they'd eat it with their bread. I passed a remark about it when I came home and one of my uncles said, 'We've got one working with us on the railway and that's what he fetches for his snack.' And they'd have dried fish. You'd often see it hanging up outside to dry; and they'd eat that.

There was a roller skating rink just down from [the warehouse] and quite a few of us used to go there. The chap who was running it had one record, *The Yellow Rose of Texas*, and we could hear it back at the billet. He used to play it over and over and over again; and one of the times when we went, we said it to him. He just said, 'I play it 'cos I like it.' You'd say, 'Oh no, not again,' when it came on; and I still do it now – it's like being back there again!

Sometimes we went down into Brussels itself and there was the Metropolitan Cinema. We used to go there; and once or twice there was an American band on and we were allowed to go to that. It was a live band, American service men, and we used to listen to them. We got invited to one or two army camps at Ostend. They used to send a truck for us, we'd go and then they'd fetch us back. Then they'd move on, and another lot would come in, and we'd get invited to them. There used to be notice up saying there's a dance at such-and-such and if we wanted to, we'd go. When we went there, we weren't really working because we had a month there while they sorted out where we finally had to go. It was more or less like a holiday.

When I was at home for ten days before [going abroad] I didn't know where I was going. Mam and I agreed that when I was writing, I could put something in so she'd know if I was in Germany, or Belgium, or wherever. Anyway, before we went, we knew where we were going so I was able to let them know.

It was a good time, really, considering that war was still raging. It was different to what we'd been used to, but it was good.

Miss Mabel Newton

In 1939, when war was threatened, Mabel Newton was still at school in Manchester, and she was due to be evacuated to Lytham St Anne's on the north-west coast. Because she was concerned about her elderly parents, she opted not to go. She left school at the end of the summer term and went to work a fortnight before the outbreak of war. Her job became a reserved occupation. At that time, Manchester's cotton industry was still very active, and so there were many ancillary factories and services that were connected with it, one of which Mabel joined. The company she worked for made dyestuffs which were used for myriad purposes, not least the production of uniforms for the armed forces.

My best subject at school was science; it was actually chemistry. I went for an interview for a post with a Swiss firm that had a [plant] in Manchester. I met a girl at the interview, who remained a friend for the rest of my life, and she and I were taken on, but we weren't in the same laboratories.

Every single piece of material that came into the firm had to be tested. They were primarily organic dyestuffs and heavy chemicals [that we were dealing with]. They had never employed women in the work; it was dangerous: below the laboratories we had this railway line full of tankers, there were chemicals in the air, chemicals that you handled; they were having problems, even then, that too

many of the men were developing cancer which they presumed was from the carcinogenic chemicals.

The boilers were needed for steam and heat [and] had to be kept going all year round. They were called Lancashire boilers and were enormous things, and they had to be fuelled with special coal which must not have any stone or ash. Once a year they closed the firm, closed the boilers and raked them out; that was called the Wakes

Week, so you always had at least a week's holiday while the boilers
were cleaned out. The firm was at a standstill, and you went off to
Blackpool, or wherever it was you went to.

One of the laboratories tested all the incoming stuff, so that meant
every acid, every bit of coal for the boilers, every salt that was
brought in. There was a smaller laboratory that tested everything that
went out, and I was in that laboratory. Everything that was being
bought had to be tested to a high standard. I tested all sorts of
dyestuffs, and I also worked in a little separate laboratory for testing
foodstuffs' colours. Foodstuffs' dyes were becoming big in those days,
and they might have arsenic, lead, zinc and manganese, which all had
to be tested for, and had to be at a very minimal amount. The raw
material was going out of this firm, but then it would be purified, in
Surrey, actually because this Swiss firm had another place [there], to
be used in foodstuffs. Because the names were so long, chemically, I
had a row of bottles on a shelf which would read *Pea Green, Raspberry
Red, Egg Yellow,* etc.

To get down to the metals themselves, you had what was called a
kjeldahl flask and a Bunsen burner, and you had to put the material
into strong sulphuric acid in the kjeldahl flask, heat it up and then
you had to drip nitric acid onto it down the long neck of the
kjeldahl flask. This was done in a fume cupboard with just your arm
inside, but whereas now you have protective clothes and holes in the
wall of the fume cupboard, you didn't have [then], so you almost lost
all the skin on that hand; it just peeled off. So you only did a month
of it.

Not having had women there before, all the men in the analytical
laboratories were treading on eggshells; everything was very, very
stiff. And it was all very new to me; I'd never been in an industrial
plant at all. I learnt soon afterwards that they'd all been told 'No
jokes, No swearing, Be on your best behaviour, Don't let her carry
a 10 litre bottle up from the downstairs lab'. But that, of course,
produced problems because as the boys came in to fill the places of
the men that went [to war], they had to do these extra jobs, so they
thought they ought to get a little bit more money.

All the material that came in had to be sampled. In order to
sample oleum, which is extremely strong sulphuric acid, you had to
stand on top of a tanker, with a long glass pole, put it down into the
tanker, put your thumb on top, bring it up and then fill your bottle.

If you got spotted with it, you got a very, very nasty burn. Accidents very often happened.

Because they were a Swiss firm, they were found at one stage to be making dyestuffs for the [German] uniforms which they couldn't get in Germany at the time; of course, another well-known British chemical company were doing the same thing, even though it was in the middle of the war. But Switzerland was neutral, so the goods went into Switzerland and out into Germany. It was discovered and stopped! No senior post was given to a British person. They always brought German–Swiss [people] in for those [positions]. They had a big research [facility], and they did small runs to see if [a process] would work on a bigger scale; and they had a lovely big library in this laboratory block.

I went to night school, which was paid for by the firm, and I went with a German girl who was living in Britain. They wouldn't allow her to continue her studying of science; she had to go and do sewing machining. She was trying to continue her studies in the group that we were with, but without the practical background it was almost impossible for her. I don't know what happened to her, but she didn't last very long. But it didn't matter whether it was the German people in Britain, or the Japanese in California, there have always been problems with these people who are trapped there.

The work changed because of the war. We used dynamite in our armaments but the French preferred cordite. If you take something like trinitrotoluene which is TNT, and set it off, it'll give an initial explosion but that releases the nitrate part of the 'trinitro' which becomes nitric acid and which then sops up the rest, so you get an initial explosion, but then it doesn't carry on. So, in order to make it work for a longer time, whatever the explosive used is, you have to have a material that sops up the nitric acid. The material that the British used was gun cotton.[15] The French [used] a chemical called centralite, so the firm built in the centre [a place] to make it for the French, although it was under what we now call the MOD. It had to be done under special observation, it had to be sealed correctly with a proper seal, and it was picked up and taken away by the MOD from the laboratory when they took the testing bottles. I don't know how they'd take it – on the railway, I presume. It wasn't explosive, you see; it was when you put the explosive in it that it was used. I did the testing of the centralite.

Once, the centralite factory went afire and it could've been a dreadful disaster because they made the centralite from chlorine which was brought in in big containers, gas cylinders. The men were trying to carry the gas cylinders out of the fire area, and they managed to get the cylinders out without any of them bursting. They were red hot and the sheer danger if one of them had gone up! If a few of them had gone up, the whole of eastern Manchester would've been gassed. About eight people got commendations for that.

There was a sudden call-up of the men and the women came in their hundreds outside the firm trying to get the work that the men had done. At first [the firm] didn't know what to do, but then they started taking the women on. I could watch the women from my window pushing enormous tipper trolleys full of salt; really quite heavy work, but it was so important for them to have money. I wasn't involved with them, but the firm then took on quite a big force of women labourers doing these sorts of heavy jobs that the men did, even shovelling salt into the outside settlement tanks for the dyes. They were very glad to have the women in the end.

Manchester had raid after raid after raid, primarily because it had a very big industrial section called Trafford Park – there were munition areas down there – and so the planes were always directed to that. The way the planes would come across would [be to] follow the railway lines. The firm I worked for was on the east side of Manchester, and although there was a very big electric power station up the road with four of these big steam [chimneys], great concrete things, and there was also the gas works with great big gasometer things which, if they'd hit them, would have caused awful disaster, the Germans accepted that Trafford Park was the target to keep going for. It was amazing really because, in all the seven years I was with that firm, they were hit with only one incendiary and it didn't go off. Incredible.

I remember on the nights of 22/23 and 23/24 December 1940 there were very heavy raids on Manchester; Liverpool and Belfast got it too. They were hit with incendiaries, and Liverpool had asked for help with extra fire engines on the first night. That meant Manchester had very few engines to cope with the fires the next night when the second wave came over. The company had its own fire engines, and so they did what they could to help out.

When you came into the works, the rather posh offices were on one side of the road, and a place called the dye house where they actually used the dyes to check the colours; it was all very clinical on that side. The real works bit was on the right hand side and it had a public house on the corner, a real old-fashioned British pub, where the men were allowed to go and have a couple of drinks at their lunch hour, because they were dealing with all these [chemicals] and the air was thick. You went down for about 200 yards and then you came to the weigh lodge for the trucks that came in because everything had to be weighed. The railway line also came in through the weigh lodge area, and it had a siding that ran off, on a more hilly area that was also a sort of slag heap which they called the mucky mountain. As soon as the war started, part of the forces, the local territorials I suppose they were – and they were well equipped – were posted on this mucky mountain. There was talk of bringing body bags there and putting [them] in part of the store room area, should they have a need. You had a works pass with your photograph on for security so you really felt as though you were in the middle of a war. Even from the very beginning, whether you were professional or otherwise, everybody had to

A lab like the one in which Mabel Newton worked.

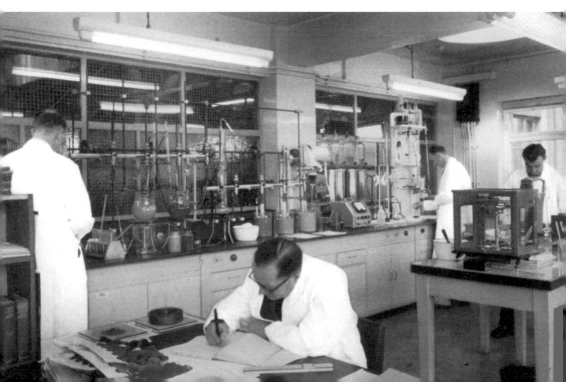

clock on. We had a clock that you had to write your name on – it wasn't one for sticking tickets in – you had to write your name on the reel on the clock and then move the handle over. It was important because everybody in the firm was given a bonus which depended on your punctuality and on your manager's report of you.

There was a sampling department and anybody new to the firm, except the women, had to do a stint in the sampling department. It was a pity, really, that the women weren't allowed to do it because you never got the complete insight into the workings. You could see the sampling going on outside the laboratory windows, on top of these tankers. We had a little area beyond our lab where the samples that had been finished with had to be emptied, tipped away, and then the jars rewashed. We used part of that area for doing distillations.

The firm were always anxious to help with the forces, so in their staff canteen they held dances every now and again, and they would invite parties of whoever was in the local barracks; they'd send out tickets. Then they'd ask us because there were very few girls really. It was interesting – the firm itself had been completely men-orientated and, of course, the war forced the women [in]. I am so grateful to it because it put me in a career which many women at that time were not able to do. You did find as the war went on that women were taken into the factories doing factory-type of jobs, but once the war finished, their jobs finished too.

When I was eighteen, I went three nights a week to the Manchester College of Technology. When the air raids became very bad, we had to move the night school to the weekends because you got air raids at night, but not so much in the daytime. So we went on Saturday afternoon and all day Sunday. We worked [in the lab on] Saturday mornings – that was expected of you. The College of Technology was six floors high and we were on the fifth floor. If there was an air raid we had to go down into the cellar, or we could leave. If it was near to 9 o'clock quite often we would leave and try and get home. It was entirely up to the bus or tram drivers whether they continued their service or not. So I've been on buses that have taken me half the way there and the bus driver would come and say, 'I'm not going any further – you'll all have to get out and go and find a shelter!'

Immediately there was an air raid, there was always a circle of barrage balloons put up to get the planes to go higher, otherwise they got tangled in the wires and so on. There were always groups of ack-ack gunners to fire at the bombers coming over, and there were searchlight groups usually near to the barrage balloons, so you could get the sky absolutely lit up with the beams from the searchlights. Once I was walking home in this situation and there was a plane that had these 1,000lb parachute bombs that were in drums like dustbins. They would drop slowly, and they wouldn't go into the ground; whatever they touched would set them off so if they touched a high building . . .

A plane came over as the three of us were walking down this road, and we could suddenly see that these parachute bombs were being dropped. A chap was running down the road and he grabbed hold of me and said, 'Get down in the gutter – quickly!' and he pushed me down and was almost on top of me, and the others were doing the same. We could watch the parachute bomb from our lying position. It came down and the parachute caught on a tree and the bomb was just hanging, swinging, but it didn't go off. When we realised it was fine, we got up and then we ran because we knew there was a shelter at the end of this road, about half a mile length down the road. When we got to the shelter, which would've held about 100 people, it had been bombed.

I remember one Christmas there was one present I had to buy, a pair of gloves from a shop in Manchester Piccadilly. I had to work on the Saturday morning so I cycled to work to avoid problems later. The trolley bus went almost into Manchester but no further. I knew a back street into the centre, where the drays were taken, under the arches of the London-Manchester-Glasgow railway line. I ran along this road, Store Street, and suddenly at the bottom end of Manchester Piccadilly everything was a wreck: buildings had collapsed and there were fires everywhere. Portland Street was a prime area of offices for cotton firms in Victorian buildings, and it had a gas main with flames two feet wide [66cm] shooting across the street. I went to the shop for these gloves and was surprised to find it was still there, but not a window was left. There was broken glass all over the displays, which were still on the stands. The shop was open! I bought the gloves and went back the way I'd come, through huge numbers of people cleaning up, workmen and so on.

On Saturday nights I worked at quite a big canteen on Manchester Victoria station, and it was an absolute eye-opener. Manchester Victoria station had a very long platform that joined it up with Manchester Exchange station, and the trains came through at night with the forces on them. Sometimes they stopped for only ten minutes and you suddenly had 300 – 500 men: 'Cup of tea and a sandwich, Miss', and the sandwich was always a cheese sandwich. We had two enormous urns: tea at one side and coffee down at the bottom end. They were in continuous use and the floor along by the counter got so terribly wet with the drips we always had chunks of cardboard that were put on the floor, and that got wet. Somebody was always grating cheese for the sandwiches. We had to cut the bread which didn't come sliced and they were very big loaves. We had a bacon slicer which nobody was allowed to touch except the senior who was in charge that night. We also had a side of bacon and that was for breakfasts, and it had to be sliced on the bacon slicer. We had a toaster that took 12 pieces of this sliced bread and, believe me, all the time you were pulling in and out and turning over the toast – you couldn't help but get singed bread at times! Very occasionally you got things like sausages, but eggs were very scarce, particularly in the winter months. The canteen was very active until about two in the morning, so there were some mattresses in the back and if you were really tired, you could go and lie down till about half-past four. There were mice around, and steam flies, all sorts of insect life lived there!

The white Americans who came into the canteen were dreadful to the black Americans, and you'd have confrontation the moment that they were coming along the counters to get what they wanted. There would be unpleasantness; there'd even be spitting – it was all very unpleasant. The powers-that-be realised this problem and had to make a separate [place] for the black personnel. It was something that I don't ever want to experience again.

It was very interesting because you also had a lot of military police on the station picking up people they were [suspicious] of. We were all instructed to watch the uniforms and check the badges, and I got involved with a chap who was in the musical corps who had a very unusual uniform. My friend and I started at 10 o'clock one Saturday night. This particular chap came in very late and my friend was very concerned – she was really up on the [uniforms]. We talked with him and talked about his uniform and so on. He said he was a musician and played in a band. He was British and in a slightly darker khaki uniform, but the whole set of [it] was not right. Ordinary soldiers had battle dress, and all the shoulder [pips] and cap badges, and so on, but he had very little of that. He did have a sort of Sam Browne[16] but not a real one. He could see that we weren't believing him, so he said, 'You come and see my band on Monday night'. My friend's boyfriend was very worried about us going to this NAAFI club, which no out-of-uniform person was allowed to enter; he was concerned that it was a pick-up, as was his friend, who I knew and quite liked. But we went, and the two boys went with us. We were met at the door by a soldier who took us in. The chap saw us and walked us along, and was introducing us, taking our coats for us, and so on. Somebody enquired who we were, and he said, 'Oh, they sing with the band – they've had to be at another venue until now, but they've come up to join the band now'. So here's my friend and I thinking, 'My God, we can't sing a note really', and he said, 'Don't worry, don't worry – it'll be alright'. He plucked a couple of chaps from the side and asked them to look after us, and take us onto the dance floor, and so on. But it was very obvious he was the band leader and there was no problem. Eventually, we came out again, and the two boys were still there, waiting outside.

There was one night when a German plane that had been hit was coming down. It was dropping stick bombs right across the line of our houses and they hit the boys' school just beyond, and a house further back. I was in bed at the time, and it's the only time that I couldn't move – I was absolutely petrified. It did come down, and it was very, very close. It dropped all the bombs – they used to release the bombs and then it would travel on for about two miles and then come down.

I was having my senior maths exam on May 8, which was the day when the European war was declared [over], so everybody was given the day off, and the exam was cancelled. We went into Manchester, and the atmosphere in the city centre was wonderful, although I wasn't involved in street parties or things of that kind. It did mean there was release – you could travel once again, and in the summer of 1945, I went across to Belfast, which was very interesting.

1 The Pioneer Corps was an army combatant force used for light engineering tasks. For more information, see http://www.royalpioneercorps.co.uk

2 A hover is a brooder with a canopy, to keep warm air close to the ground to warm the chicks, and is usually suspended from the ceiling.

3 Rudge Whitworth Cycles was a British bicycle and motorcycle manufacturer formed as the result of a merger of two bicycle manufacturers in 1894, one of which descended from the original bicycle company founded by Daniel Rudge. For more information, see http://www.rudge.co.uk

4 Toad of Toad Hall from *A Wind in the Willows* by Kenneth Graham.

5 Tessie O'Shea was a Welsh entertainer and actress well known for her large size. For more information, see http://tessie.sea-sounds.com/

6 Leaf is the highest grade of lard, obtained from the fat deposit surrounding the kidneys and inside the loin. It has little pork flavour, making it ideal for use in baked goods.

7 Scratchings are bits of the skin of a pig fried until crisp, and salted, eaten for a snack.

8 *Workers' Playtime* was a simple comedy and music radio show designed to raise the morale of the workers, and to encourage them to greater effort. For more information, see http://www.whirligig-tv.co.uk/radio/workersplaytime.htm

9 Henry Hall was a band leader who played from the 1920s-50s. For more information see http://en.wikipedia.org/wiki/Henry_Hall_(bandleader)

10 Plymouth was bombed from April 1940 to July 1944, the dockyards being the main target. For more information see http://en.wikipedia.org/wiki/Plymouth_Blitz

11 The Dutch East Indies is now Indonesia. Lascars were Indian soldiers or sailors who worked for the Dutch government.

12 The *Marnix St Aldegonde* was attacked by German aircraft on 6 November 1943 in the Mediterranean, and sank with no loss of life. For another personal account, see http://www.burmastar.org.uk/marnix.htm

13 The Palais du Centenaire was one of the buildings designed for the World's Fair of 1935.

14 Women who fraternised with Germans had their hair shaved, and they were shunned by the communities in which they lived.

15 For more information about gun cotton and its applications, see http://en.wikipedia.org /wiki/Nitrocellulose

16 Sam Browne is the leather belt worn by officers in the army. It goes around the waist and across one shoulder.

Chapter 5

Special Operations Executive – SOE

This book concludes with the story of women who paid the ultimate price for their active service. Denise Bloch, a young Jewish woman who joined the SOE, was sent to France; Violette Szabó who also served in France, and whose story was immortalised in the film *Carve Her Name with Pride* and Princess Noor Khan, who was executed in Dachau camp.

The SOE was a British secret war department formed in 1940 to 'Set Europe Ablaze' by organising and supplying the underground Resistance movements against the Nazis (and later the Japanese) in all occupied countries. It was one of several secret armies commanded from London by General Colin Gubbins, who was vice chair of its council; the chairman was the banker Charles Hambro, until succeeded by Gubbins in September 1943. The French section of SOE, however, was commanded by Colonel Maurice Buckmaster, a Dunkirk veteran, working from secret offices at Marks and Spencer's headquarters in Baker Street, London.

This section infiltrated 39 women into France by plane, boat, submarine and parachute between May 1941 and July 1944. Whichever service they were recruited from – WAAFs, ATS, etc. – the women were often enlisted into the First Aid Nursing Yeomanry (FANYs) in order to go some way towards complying with the Geneva Convention that women in the services should not bear arms, though this was not consistently practised by SOE. Of these 39 women, 15 were captured and only three of these survived. Of the 12 murdered by the Nazis, one was the Jewish agent Denise Bloch and a thirteenth girl, Jewish agent Muriel Byck[1] died of meningitis after six weeks of intense work in the field, on 23 May 1944. The Free French section sent in a further 11 girls from the *Corps Auxilière Feminin* or French ATS, all of whom survived, making a total of 50 women who served in France.

Jewish participation in the hazardous war of the SOE was – as in all theatres of the war – far out of proportion to the community's numbers in the general population. Some of the Jewish SOE agents are quite well known: Captain Adam Rabinovich ('Arnaud'), *Croix de Guerre*, murdered by the Gestapo; Captain Isadore Newman ('Julien' / 'Pepe'), MBE, murdered at Mauthausen camp; Captain Maurice Pertschuck, MBE ('Martin Perkins' / 'Eugene'), murdered at Buchenwald camp. In addition, hundreds of other Jews fought with SOE agents in the resistance groups of occupied countries, especially in France and Poland.

Denise Bloch: 'Ambroise'

Ensign F/27 Denise Madeleine Bloch (codename Ambroise) First Aid Nursing Yeomanry, SOE, received the King's Commendation for Brave Conduct, the *Legion d'Honneur*, the *Croix de Guerre avec Palme* and *Médaille de la Résistance avec Rosette*. Denise was murdered by the Nazis at Ravensbrück concentration camp near Mecklenburg together with Violette Szabó, GC (see below), and Lilian Rolfe[2], *Croix de Guerre*, some time between 25 January and 2 February 1945. Denise, who had three brothers, was French but served in the British Forces. Aged 29 years, she was the daughter of the Parisian Jewish family of Jacques Henri and Suzanne Barrault née Lévi-Strauss. She is commemorated at Brookwood Commonwealth War Graves Cemetery, Surrey (panel 26, column 3); on a separate plaque with Szabó, Rolfe and [Cecily] Lefort [née MacKenzie][3]; on the FANY memorial on the wall of St Paul's Church, Wilton Place, Knightsbridge; on a plaque at Ravensbrück concentration camp itself; and on the F (France) Section memorial at Valençay in France, unveiled in May 1991 by the late Queen Mother.

Denise has been described as being 'broad shouldered and blonde' but her service photograph reveals a dark haired beauty. She in fact dyed her hair blonde in France as the police had raided her flat in Lyons and had stolen photographs of her with her black hair.

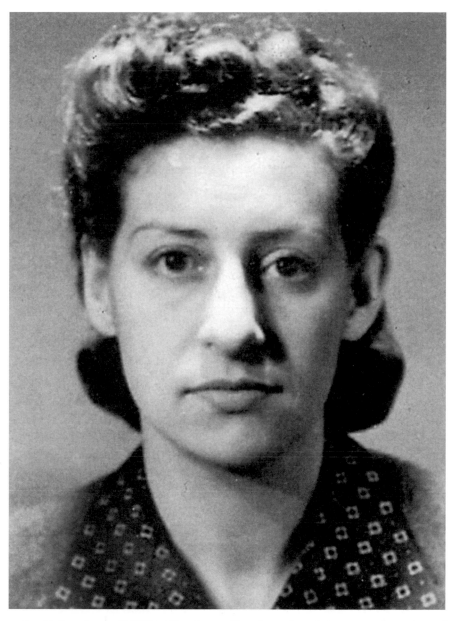

In F Section of SOE, Denise enlisted under the assumed name of Danielle Williams, though some SOE documents insist on spelling her real name as 'Block'. Vera Atkins, squadron and intelligence officer in SOE, F Section and personal assistant and Number 2 to Buckmaster, remembers her as tall and sturdy and also argumentative, but explains this trait as being due to the fact that she had already had a lot of experience in the resistance in France before her exit to England (see below) and knew better than her trainers what Nazi occupation really meant.

The archives of the Special Forces Club in London and the SOE files reveal that Denise and her family were living in Lyons where she worked as secretary to Lieutenant Jean Maxime Aron (codename Joseph), an employee of Citroën, and a Jewish resistance leader. She was engaged to Dominique Mendelsohn (himself an agent) but this was allegedly an engagement of convenience to assist her work. She was recruited in July 1942 in Lyons by Monsieur René Piercy (codename Adolphe/Étienne) and in turn she recruited her 'fiancé'! Denise worked first in circuit 'Detective', commanded by Captain Henri Paul Sevenet (codename Rodolphe), with the wireless operator (W/O) Captain Brian J. Stonehouse (codename Célestin), who died on 2 December 1998. As well as being a courier, she was meant to look after and accompany Stonehouse, whose French was not too good.

In her London debriefing on 11 June 1943, Denise described how she saw Stonehouse in the street in Lyons with two men on 24 October 1942, followed them and saw that he was taken to a police station: she realised he had been arrested. Stonehouse was good at drawing and always had his sketch book (which Denise often carried), despite Denise's warnings to him not to carry such incriminating items with him. He also once addressed her loudly in the street in English and said, 'After the war you must come to Scotland to see my house'. Denise alleged he was homesick and too young for his job. Curiously, Stonehouse's debrief document does not mention Denise at all, for some inexplicable reason, and yet he clearly worked closely with her for some time.

Being in danger, following Stonehouse's arrest, she left for Marseilles on 26 October. Whilst there, she was sent to a rendezvous at her hotel to receive secret papers about landing grounds and other matters from agent L'Allemand at 7pm on the evening of 31 October. The next day he was arrested but she could not explain to her debriefers why this had happened. From Marseilles she volunteered to return to Lyons with the papers she had been given, instead of Aron, but he and Sevenet insisted on accompanying her because she was a woman alone. However, unknown to them, they had been betrayed to the Gestapo and Aron was arrested at the station near the small entrance, by a Gestapo group that had his photograph from a raid on his flat. (He later escaped and got back to Britain on 26 July 1944.) Sevenet was right behind Aron but slipped through. Denise also evaded capture by accidentally leaving by the main exit, and she and Sevenet were met by Amedée Contran. All three then went into hiding in St Laurent de Chamousset near Lyons on 3 November 1942, in the house of Madame St Victor.

Denise admitted to having sent a cable to her mother (which had been intercepted by the police) in Lyons. The police had searched the mother's flat finding nothing, but the cable may have been the reason why the police were waiting at the station in Lyons for her and her two comrades. However, the Gestapo were expecting Denise to arrive with Aron and so missed her, by sheer good fortune, when Aron left the station alone.

Denise then moved to Villefranche-sur-Mer on 10 November, 1942, remaining in hiding and out of action until January 1943. She made only one trip, to Nice to get her hair dyed. She then moved to Toulouse, and Sevenet introduced her to Sergeant Maurice Dupont of circuit 'Diplomat' who was [supposed] to help her cross from Oloron-St-Marie, into Spain and out of danger. However, deep snow and enemy patrols prevented this and they had to return to Toulouse.

In Toulouse they met Colonel George Reginald Starr (codenamed Hilaire/Gaston) of circuit 'Wheelwright' who took her to work in Agen with Philippe de Vomecourt. After two other Jewish SOE agents, Lieutenant Maurice Pertschuk (codename Eugène) and his W/O Lieutenant Marcus Bloom (codename Urbain), were arrested in April 1943, Starr decided to send Denise to London as his courier, with Dupont, as they now had no wireless transmission facility. Denise knew and had met Pertschuk several times whilst carrying messages between Toulouse and Agen, and described him at their meetings as often dishevelled and worried, seeing him last on 12 April for their usual lunch together. The following week Pertschuk did not arrive for his lunch appointment. She and Starr waited in vain at an agreed safe address and made inquiries, but later they discovered that Pertschuk had been arrested the next day (13 April). Yet again Denise had had a very close shave!

In her London debrief, Denise gave much useful information, describing, for example, how there were many young men who were constantly picked up on the street by gendarmes and Gestapo for labour work in Germany, warning that agents sent to France in future should therefore not look too young, or they will often be stopped automatically and arrested. She also emphasised to SOE that future agents must speak excellent French, for anyone suspected of having a foreign accent was deported at once to Germany. In addition she described how the Gestapo agents spoke such good French, many having lived there for 20 years or more that you did not know if you were talking to a French national or a German.

Denise went on to graphically describe how on one occasion she was carrying her radio in the usual suitcase pack when about to travel on a bus. She saw a Gestapo inspection in progress at the bus stop, so she engaged one of the Gestapo in poor German, causing him some amusement, and asked him to hold her case whilst she bought a newspaper. She then showed her papers to a civilian inspector, returned for her case and got coolly on the bus with no trouble – something out of a wartime movie.

She also related how she and Sevenet found by chance a sympathiser contact in the *Deuxième Bureau* (French Internal Security) who would issue agents with forged *cartes d'identité*.

Denise and Dupont finally left Agen on 29 April via Toulouse and Montréjeau, where they spent the night, and then travelled for three hours by train, 17 kilometres to Cier de Luchon, on the first stage of the journey to get to Britain. Starr had promised her a route out of the country of only three kilometres on flat ground. At Cier, she told the *chef de gare* she had urgent papers to get through to Britain. He said she was mad and there were six hundred yards and several patrols to pass before reaching the hotel where she could get 'help'; but they went on and met no Germans. The proprietor of the Hôtel des Trois Ormeaux found her a room for the day until he arranged two *passeurs* for the price of five thousand francs, to get her over the Pyrenees. She left at half an hour after midnight, and after 15 hours hiking across the Pyrenees at 3,300 metres, with bare legs and a half-length coat (at one point her guides stopped and made her a fire to warm by), they reached Bausen at 3pm on a Saturday. Here she had to wait three days for the bus, but was glad to be able to rest.

The Spanish police, meanwhile, confiscated all her papers including Colonel Starr's report. She then proceeded via Veille to Lerida, arriving on 5 May, where she met the British Consul from Barcelona and had dinner with him. He gave her documents to proceed to Madrid (8 May), where she stayed for five days and in her hotel met four escaped Allied airmen, two American and two British. From Madrid, Denise continued to Gibraltar (Saturday 15 May) for three days, then Lisbon and then ultimately to London, arriving on 21 May 1943, after a 22-day journey.

There she gave her report verbally to SOE underlining the lack of arms, money, wireless transmitters, and general stores such as clothes and food, of which Starr was especially short. She also warned that Starr asked that the SOE should be careful to whom they supplied arms as some Resistance groups were left-wing and may attempt to take power after the Nazis were ejected.

Denise's debriefers commented afterwards that she was very anxious to return to Lyons to work, but SOE warned her that she was almost certainly by now known to the Gestapo. She disagreed and said that if it was so, then Starr also needed to be brought out as they were often seen together. She added that as she had been at the same address for months, the Gestapo would have picked her up by now. She also told her debriefers that she had managed to meet her mother for a meal three months [earlier], and that she had alternative *cartes d'identité* in the names of Katrine Bérnard and Chantal Baron.

Denise now proceeded to formal training for ten months as a W/O and parachutist with SOE in Britain, and was enlisted as a FANY Ensign. F Section training began at Wanborough Manor near Guildford for those who had passed the first, stiff interviews in London. From here they continued to Arisaig House in Inverness-shire, for training on arms and explosives. Those requiring very specialist instruction, industrial sabotage, wireless, and so on, continued to specified specialist centres round the country. Then came parachute training at Ringway, near Manchester, whilst living at Tatton Park, and finally security training, use of safe houses, letter boxes and so on, at Beaulieu in Hampshire. For SOE in general, however, there were as many as 50 training schools up and down the country, mostly in isolated country houses.

At her initial training school, the following comments were written about Denise's progress: 'An experienced woman with knowledge of the world. She has courage and determination and a thorough understanding and hatred of the Boche. Has complete self assurance and is capable of handling most situations. Has a feeling of physical inferiority which limits her athletic activities. Keen to get back into the field and under a good male organiser would make a very good W/T operator or courier. Is not physically suited to the training of Group A (i.e. paramilitary training)'.

Vera Atkins recalls one of Denise's final pre-mission briefings at a commonly-frequented secret location used on such occasions, in an SOE flat at 6 Orchard Court, Portman Square, as well as the final kitting-out in authentic tailor-made French clothes. Denise also met Leo Marks,

MBE (the Chief Cryptographer, *Chef de Codage*, at SOE throughout most of the war), in February 1944, for a code briefing and was given her 'code poem' by him which he had composed.

Denise returned to work in France on the night of 2-3 March 1944 with Captain Robert Benoist (codename Lionel), landed by an RAF Westland Lysander at Soucelles, [in the Loire]. The secret drop was codenamed 'Laburnum'. Her circuit (or *réseaux*), called 'Clergyman', was a large one consisting of 2000 armed members of the *Forces Françaises de l'Intérieur* (FFI) which had to be re-established after its collapse the year before. One source alleges that the plane was met by resistance leader and former pilot Clément Rémy (codename Marc). Denise had returned to France now running the double risk of being an official SOE agent and Jewish.

Her orders were to act as courier, encoder and W/O, and assist in the attack on high pylons over the River Loire at Île Heron, and cut railway and telephone lines converging on Nantes, before D-Day, to disrupt German communications. Benoist's orders were that Denise 'will be under your command but it must be understood that she is the ultimate judge in all questions regarding the technicalities and w/t and w/t security. She will encode the messages herself...and it is of the utmost importance that her time on the air should be reduced to the minimum'. She contacted London within two weeks, on 15 March and worked for three months sending 31 messages and receiving 52.

Benoist, a wealthy racing driver, was sadly captured on 18 June 1944 in Paris visiting his dying mother and was hung later at Buchenwald concentration camp. Denise was captured the day after, following a Gestapo raid on a château belonging to the Benoist family (Villa Cécile) in Rambouillet at Sermaise, west of Paris, where she was based, with agent Jean-Paul Wimmelle, who managed to escape.

Vera Atkins said that it was clear there had been a betrayal, and they knew immediately she was captured by a message from their agents; but it would never be known now who was involved unless it was possible to scour the German documents on the issue. Nazi spies and sympathisers were rife in France at the time and so such incidents were commonplace. Only the German archives might reveal how the Gestapo knew of the presence of the SOE agents at the château, and so who the informers were, but then SOE had neither the ability nor time to get to the truth whilst the war had to be won.

After the German surrender, SOE was wound up very quickly (1 January 1946) and as it was felt that no good could come of finding the traitors – and with the turmoil in post-war Europe – matters like these were often left uninvestigated and unsolved.

As the Allies approached Paris, the Germans were forced to move all their prisoners further east and into Germany. Imprisoned at the infamous jail in Fresnes, 12 miles south of Paris, Denise was taken to Gare de l'Est by coach on 8 August with Szabó and Rolfe. They had all been in Fresnes prison at the same time, but unknown to each other. A report written by Vera Atkins, when seconded to the Judge Advocate General's Branch HQ BAOR, 13 March 1946, mentions that Denise had also been seen in interrogation centres at both 3, Place des États-Unis and the notorious 84 Avenue Foch, in Paris, the Gestapo headquarters.

Each prisoner was given a small parcel by the Red Cross, enough to last for two days. Their third class railway wagon was attached to the end of a heavily-guarded train carrying 300 German wounded as well as male prisoners. The women prisoners, separated from the men, were chained by the ankles in pairs. Vera Atkins's report states that other SOE agents on the train with them included Major Henry Peulevé and Squadron Leader Southgate *en route* to Buchenwald. After many hours delay, the train left on that hot August late afternoon.

The following day the train was attacked and damaged by the RAF, so they had to continue the journey on trucks later that night. During this attack occurred the famous incident when Violette Szabó crawled into the male prisoner section to bring them food and water. On reaching Metz, they were billeted in stables for the night. Agent Bernard Guillot alleges he saw many women prisoners at this time whilst he was being moved between prisons and especially mentions Denise in his debrief of 12 April 1945.

From here the girls were then sent on to Gestapo HQ in Strasbourg. Later they reached Saarbrücken, where the three girls were seen by Monique Level, a French prisoner, as they arrived, with Lilian looking quite ill. Finally, they arrived at Ravensbrück after a week's brutalising journey. The date was 22 August 1944.

Details of Denise's imprisonment and death are described by EH Cookridge's *Inside SOE* [currently out of print]. The three SOE girls managed to share the same bunk in their hellish prison hut. Here they were seen by SOE agents Yvonne Baseden and Eileen Nearne*. But after three weeks at Ravensbrück (the world's largest ever prison for women), she and Szabó and Rolfe were taken to Torgau (with Nearne) on 3 September, a labour camp 120 miles south of Ravensbrück, where conditions were slightly better and they worked in a factory. Nearne said they were in good spirits, especially Violette, who was constantly planning an escape. Lilian, however, was unwell. Later, Nearne was sent elsewhere and never saw them again.

Several weeks later on 5 October they were returned to Ravensbrück. Again after two weeks on 19 October, they were moved and sent east to join an *Aussenkommando* [an external branch of a concentration camp], 300 miles away near Königsberg, labouring in heavy forestry and building work at an airfield. They travelled by truck, arriving in November 1944 and worked for three months in the harshest conditions of an east European winter, mainly with Russian and Polish POWs. Both Lilian and Denise were very unwell as a result of the ill treatment here, whereas Violette had stood up to it better. Witnesses described how all three always stuck together and showed remarkable spirit.

Violette became particularly friendly with Solange[4], whilst Lilian, increasingly ill and in the hospital, was befriended by Renée Corjon. Then on 20 January, the three agents were again returned to Ravensbrück. Solange and Corjon speculated that it might be for repatriation via Sweden or Switzerland. Little did they know that it had been decided by Berlin to carry out systematic mass executions. The Allies were fast approaching and the Germans wanted to kill prisoners who had witnessed atrocities or who were considered 'important' and constituted a 'danger' to the German State.

At Ravensbrück, Baseden saw them yet again and was shocked at their much-deteriorated health. They told Baseden that they had managed to contact some male POWs on their transport back and given them a list of agents they had seen imprisoned, hoping it would get back to London.

Baseden alleges they were optimistic about getting onto another transport, perhaps to perform lighter work outside the camp, and that a French prisoner, Mary de Moncy, who worked in the infirmary, had been able to get them some food and clothes. It was de Moncy who told Yvonne Baseden later that one day the girls had been taken to the punishment cells for solitary confinement, all three being in a poor state, and Lilian unable to walk. After a further three days they were moved to an L-shaped block of cells called the bunker, a kind of prison within the prison, and were seen by an unnamed Czech woman.

Odette Churchill, GC, describes this abominable place thus: 'A short passage with a barrel gate at the end with spikes leading to the floor and ceiling, had on one side the cheerful rooms of the SS.....the gate swung on a spring hinge and led to a flight of stairs descending to a stone underground second passage with white electric light, and cells on one side, which were all in darkness inside....the cell doors had hatches through which food was passed'.

A day or two later all three agents disappeared. After the war, it was discovered, however, that the three women were taken from their cells to the yard behind the crematorium at about 7 o'clock one evening. Denise and Lilian had been badly treated and were on stretchers; only Violette was able to walk. Camp Commandant SS Sturmbannführer Fritz Suhren read the death sentences ordered by the *Reichssicherheitshauptamt* or Reich Main Security Office (RSHA) in Berlin, with second in command Schwartzhuber present. SS Sergeant Zappe guarded the girls whilst this was done. SS Sergeant Schulte (or Schulter), a block leader from the men's camp, then shot each girl in the back of the neck with a small calibre gun, as SS Corporal Schenk (in charge of the crematorium) brought them forward and held them as they knelt down. Camp doctor SS Sturmbannführer Trommer certified the deaths and the clothed bodies were removed singly by internees, and immediately cremated. The camp dentist, Dr Martin Hellinger, was there to remove any gold teeth.

Suhren was arrested by the Americans on 3 May whilst bringing Odette Churchill from Ravensbrück to the American lines, as a mitigating offering. He escaped, was recaptured, escaped again for two years, was recaptured again in 1949 by the British when he was found working in a brewery. He was then handed over to the French, [who] tried and then executed him in, ironically, Fresnes prison. The dentist received 15 years in prison, was released in 1951 and practised in Germany for years afterwards.

For months after the war, it was unofficially believed that the three girls had been liberated by the Russians and that they were possibly on their way home via Siberia, or even Sweden. This had happened before to some survivors of the German camps. A document in the SOE files, however, dated 28 April 1945, states that SOE believed the three girls were still at Ravensbrück. Then in April 1946 a newspaper story about the missing girls was seen by Mrs Julie Barry living at Joyce Grove, Nettlebed in Oxfordshire. She was a Guernsey woman who had been deported to Ravensbrück and allegedly forced to become a Kapo (No.

39785) in the *Strafeblock*. Barry was in fact a Jewish refugee who had arrived in Guernsey in July 1939 as Julia Brichta, and in April 1942 married a local man Jeremiah Barry. However, she was denounced by local Guernsey residents and deported to Ravensbrück via France on 5 May 1944.

When interviewed by two War Office officials, Barry's story was that she saw the three girls at Ravensbrück in rags, faces black with dirt and hair matted, spoke to them and gave them food and clothing. She especially remembered Violette Szabó. But her story cannot be confirmed. Another British POW at Ravensbrück was Mary Lindell. [She affirmed] that the usual method of execution there was by hanging, and she had it on reliable authority from others in the camp that the girls' clothes were returned to the stores intact after execution. Baseden, however, disputes this based on information from Mary de Moncy, who said their clothes were never returned. We will probably never know the truth of the manner of their death.

Meanwhile, Vera Atkins went to Germany on her own initiative and got herself attached to the Nuremburg War Crimes Investigation team. She began conducting inquiries in Germany on all missing agents. On 13 March 1946, at Minden prison, she found and interviewed Obersturmführer Johann Schwartzhuber, SS, the second in command (*Schutzhaftlagerführer* or Camp Overseer) at Ravensbrück, and previously a prominent prison guard at Auschwitz.

After some strong words from Atkins, a guilty-looking Schwartzhuber admitted that the three women had been brought back from Königsberg and put in the cells at Ravensbrück. He then confirmed how the girls were killed, adding that a female overseer escorted them to the crematorium yard but was sent back before the execution. He said, 'All three were very brave and I was deeply moved...we were impressed by the bearing of these women...and annoyed that the Gestapo themselves did not carry out these shootings...I recognise with certainty the photograph of Danielle Williams (Denise Bloch) and I think I recognise the photograph of Lillian Rolfe. I know that the third had the name of Violette.' The translation was confirmed by a German linguist Captain A Vollman.

Schwarzhuber also confirmed that Lilian Rolfe was unable to walk and had to be assisted to the place of execution; this was a long trek, from the cells via the kitchen, through the main gate, past the garage, to the crematorium itself. Barry insists that only Violette walked and the other two were on stretchers. Violette was shot last and had the final agony of having to watch her friends murdered in front of her.

Like Suhren (who also testified to the supreme courage and cheerfulness of the girls), Schwartzhuber was sentenced to death after his trial in Hamburg and hanged. Thus, the indefatigable Vera Atkins was only able to write letters of condolence to the girls' families in the spring of 1946, and only after this evidence from Vera Atkins, was Whitehall able to issue death certificates for the three agents, over a year after the murders.

Thus was Denise Bloch's short, brave life. Like many others, she has no known grave but her name is proudly carved on four memorials, lest we forget.

POSTSCRIPT

In 1968, Alan Rolfe, brother of Lilian Rolfe who was murdered with Denise, saw an announcement in *The Daily Telegraph* of 24 May in memory of Denise Bloch, signed 'Dave'. After enquiries at the newspaper, Dave replied to Alan Rolfe, and turned out to be Flight Lieutenant David Lomas who knew Denise when she was training in England. He was lobbying Lambeth Council to name a block of flats after her, as they had done for Rolfe and Szabó on the Vincennes Estate at Norwood, South London. However, he never succeeded: Lambeth Council claimed all the flats had been named already, and in July, Lomas was killed in an aircraft crash in the Far East, it is thought. The matter was never pursued. Perhaps it was because Denise was French, or Jewish, or both – we will never know. But Vera Atkins does confirm that perhaps there had been a romance (interview 25.4.98 East Sussex), though she pointed out that the private lives of the agents in their free time on leave from training, was their own.

(Original correspondence is in the possession of Mr Martin Sugarman, donated by Alan Rolfe to the Association of Jewish Ex-Servicemen and Women [AJEX] Museum).

The above account of Denise Bloch's life and death was, with minor amendments, reproduced by the very kind permission of Mr Martin Sugarman, author and archivist of the AJEX Military Museum. For more information about the Museum and its history, see www.ajex.org.uk   For Mr Sugarman's full account, including references and footnotes, see www.64-baker-street.org

Violette Szabó: 'Louise'

Violette Reine Elizabeth Bushell was born in Paris on the 26 June 1921. Her mother was French and her father, an Englishman from Brixton, was a motor car dealer. They had met while Violette's father was serving in France during the First World War. Her parents brought her to England, eventually settling in Stockwell, South London, where she attended school in Brixton until the age of 14. When war broke out in 1939, she was working on the perfume counter of a department store called Bon Marché.

At the Bastille Day parade in London, in 1940, Violette met Étienne Szabó, a French officer of Hungarian descent who was a career legionnaire with great leadership qualities. He led his men from the front with formidable courage in Norway, Bir Hakeim and El Alamein, and he held the *Légion d'Honneur*, the *Médaille Militaire*, the *Croix de Guerre avec toile et Palme*, and the Colonial Medal. In August, within a few weeks of meeting, Violette and Étienne were married; she was 19 years old and he was 31.

Étienne was then posted abroad and Violette did not see him for a year, until he returned for seven days leave. They met in Liverpool to spend his leave together, and Violette became pregnant. It was the last time she saw Étienne alive, as he was killed on 24 October 1942, leading his men at El Himeimat, south of El Alamein. Shortly before this, in June, Violette had given birth to a daughter, Tania, but Étienne was never to see his little girl. It was her devastation at Étienne's death that helped Violette to make the decision to volunteer for the SOE.

She had already joined the ATS in 1941, and shortly after Tania's birth, Violette received a letter from a Mr Potter. She was requested to attend an interview in London, and when she arrived, she was shown into a room with only a table and two chairs, on one of which sat Mr Potter. He suggested that her fluency in French and knowledge of France could be useful for special war work. He told her that he was seeking people to do 'dangerous work' in occupied France. Violette asked whether he meant spying, but the reply was, 'No, not spying, but similar'. The 'job description' was to undergo training, and then enter enemy-occupied territory to make life difficult for the Germans. Violette agreed immediately, but Mr Potter first wanted to check Violette's credentials with the security services; and he also wanted her to give it some serious thought. She returned a week later and gave him the same answer.

Violette cleared the security checks and, after an assessment for fluency in the French language and further interviews, she became a member of the SOE. She received intensive training in the use of weapons (both Allied and German), escape and evasion, unarmed combat, night and daylight navigation, demolition explosives, and communications and cryptography. She had a minor accident during parachute training which resulted in a delay in her deployment into the field. But, on 5 April 1944, she was parachuted into France, near Cherbourg.

Violette's codename was Louise, and one of her first tasks was to reorganise a network of French resistence that had been smashed by the

Germans. She led the new group in sabotaging road and rail bridges; and she transmitted wireless reports to SOE headquarters, on the local factories which were producing war materials for the Germans. These messages were extremely important in establishing Allied bombing targets. At one point, she was obliged to explain herself to the French police who had arrested her. Having convinced them that she was of no danger, she was freed and made her way to Paris, where she requested a pick up. She returned to England on a Westland Lysander on 30 April 1944, her first mission having been accomplished successfully.

Her second parachute drop into France was in June 1944, immediately after the Normandy landings, and she was dropped near Limoges. There she coordinated the activities of the local *Maquis* (led by Jacques Dufour) in order to sabotage the German communication lines during the enemy's attempts to halt the Normandy landings. On 10 June, she was a passenger in a car that raised the suspicions of German troops at an unexpected roadblock. Sturmbannführer Helmut Kämpfe of the *Das Reich* Division, had been captured by members of the local resistance, and the road block had been set up as part of the operation to find him. A gun battle ensued, and Violette fought valiantly using a Sten gun, until her ammunition ran out[5].

While her *Maquis* colleagues escaped unscathed in the confusion, Violette was captured and taken to the Gestapo headquarters in Limosges. There, she was intensively interrogated. She was tortured, sexually assaulted, raped and beaten severely, but she did not give away any information.

From Limoges she was transferred to the notorious Fresnes prison in Paris and from there, in early August 1944, she was sent, by train, to the concentration camp at Ravensbrück (see the account of this journey on page 205). In Ravensbrück, where over 92,000 women died, Violette was forced to do hard labour, and she suffered the severest privations. Odette Churchill, a survivor of the infamous camp described Violette as outstanding amongst the thousands of women there. Along with Denise Bloch and Lilian Rolfe, Violette was executed some time between the end of January and the beginning of February 1945.

During her training with the SOE, Violette was given a poem by Leo Marks, the head of the Codes Section, to use in her coded messages. It was written by Marks himself, who preferred not to use already-published poetry, which could be decoded more easily. Violette's poem was *The Life that I Have*.

The Life that I Have
The life that I have is all that I have
And the life that I have is yours.
The love that I have of the life that I have
Is yours and yours and yours.
The sleep I shall have, a rest I shall have
Yet death will be but a pause.
For the peace of my years in the long green grass
Will be yours and yours and yours.

Readers familiar with the film *Carve Her Name with Pride*, will remember that the poem was supposedly written by Étienne for Violette, but this was artistic licence. Nevertheless, it is a beautiful poem, and has remained famous because of its associations with Violette.

Violette was awarded the *Croix de Guerre* by the French government in 1947, and the *Médaille de la Résistance* in 1973. As one of the SOE agents who died for the liberation of France, Violette is also listed on the Roll of Honour on the SOE Memorial in the town of Valençay, in the Indre *département*. She was only the second woman to be awarded the George Cross, and her daughter, Tania, aged just four years, received her posthumously-bestowed medal on 17 December 1946.

The Citation was as follows:
St. James's Palace, SW1, 17th December, 1946
The KING has been graciously pleased to award the GEORGE CROSS to Violette, Madame SZABÓ (deceased), Women's Transport Service (First Aid Nursing Yeomanry).

Madame Szabó volunteered to undertake a particularly dangerous mission in France. She was parachuted into France in April, 1944, and undertook the task with enthusiasm. In her execution of the delicate researches entailed she showed great presence of mind and astuteness. She was twice arrested by the German security authorities but each time managed to get away. Eventually, however, with other members of her group, she was surrounded by the Gestapo in a house in the south west of France. Resistance appeared hopeless but Madame Szabó, seizing a Sten-gun and as much ammunition as she could carry, barricaded herself in part of the house and, exchanging shot for shot with the enemy, killed or wounded several of them. By constant movement, she avoided being cornered and fought until she dropped exhausted. She was arrested and had to undergo solitary confinement. She was then continuously and

Violette's daughter Tania, aged four, with the George Cross which was posthumously awarded to her mother.

atrociously tortured but never by word or deed gave away any of her acquaintances or told the enemy anything of any value. She was ultimately executed. Madame Szabó gave a magnificent example of courage and steadfastness.

Noor-un-Nisa Inayat Khan: 'Madeleine'

Noor Inayat Khan was born the eldest of four children, on 1 January 1914 in Moscow. The name Noor means 'light of womanhood', and the baby was to be known by her patronymic 'Inayat', and the title 'Khan', indicating an aristocratic birth. Noor's was a princely Indian Muslim family, descended from Tipu Sultan, the famous eighteenth century ruler of Mysore, whose great-great grandaughter Noor was. Tipu died in the battles to halt the British conquest of Southern India. Noor's father, Hazrat Inayat Khan, was a leader of the Sufti mystic community and a teacher of Sufism[6]. He was also a gifted musician. Her mother, an American from Albuquerque, New Mexico, was Ora Meena Ray Baker. Ora had met Inayat Khan when he was travelling in the United States. Her half-brother, and guardian at the time she met Hazrat Inayat Khan, was the American yogi and scholar, Pierre Bernard; and she was also related to Mary Baker Eddy, the founder of Christian Science.

Just prior to the outbreak of the First World War, the family moved to London, to Bloomsbury, and Noor attended a kindergarten in Notting Hill.

However, because of poverty and prejudice, the family moved again in 1920, this time to Suresnes near Paris. They settled into a house which

was gifted to the family by a benefactor of the Sufi movement. In 1927, when Noor was just 13 years old, her father died of influenza and, as the eldest child, it fell to her to take responsibility for both her mother, who was grief-stricken, and her younger siblings.

When she left school, Noor studied at the Sorbonne, taking a degree in child psychology. She also studied music at the Paris conservatoire, under Nadia Boulanger, composing for harp and piano; and simultaneously studied several modern languages. She was described as being quiet, shy, sensitive, and dreamy; and she gradually became more European in both her habits and dress, while wearing make-up that made her skin lighter.

She and her brother Vilayat travelled throughout continental Europe, and she began a career as a freelance writer of poetry and children's stories. She contributed many articles and stories to newspapers and magazines, and her children's fairy tales were broadcast by French radio. A book of her stories, *Twenty Játaka Tales*, was published in England in 1939. The stories were inspired by the Játaka tales of Buddhist tradition. She was about to publish a children's newspaper in Paris when war broke out.

In the early months of the war Noor decided to join the *Union de Femmes de France*, a volunteer nursing organisation, with her sister, but when France was overrun by German troops in 1940, the family fled to Bordeaux. Because Vilayat had been born in England, they managed to get on the last boat evacuating British subjects, and they landed in Falmouth on 22 June 1940.

Noor was very much a pacifist, but she decided to do what she could to help defeat the Nazi tyranny. She joined the Women's Auxiliary Air Force (WAAF), as an Aircraftwoman 2nd Class, on 19 November 1940, and was posted to Harrogate to be trained as a wireless operator. She was 26 years old.

She was posted to a bomber training school station in June 1941, but she found the work dull and boring. In an attempt to relieve her boredom, she applied for a commission, and was selected for an intensive course of more specialised and highly technical signals training. However, she thought she would not get her commission as she believed she made a poor impression on the interview board. She felt she had become too emotional about the then-problematic subject of Indian independence. Indeed, she let the panel know she passionately supported the struggle for Indian independence, to the point that, after the war, she might feel obliged to fight the British in India.

Then, quite unexpectedly, Noor was asked by the War Office to attend the Victoria Hotel in Northumberland Avenue, London, for an interview with a Captain Jepson. He told her about the shortage of wireless operators to work with British officers who were organising resistance groups in occupied France. He also made it plain there was a real risk of capture, torture and death at the hands of the Gestapo. She accepted the post.

She was later recruited to join F (France) Section of the Special Operations Executive, and in early February 1943, she was posted to the Air Ministry, Directorate of Air Intelligence, seconded to First Aid Nursing Yeomanry (FANYs). She was sent to Wanborough Manor, near Guildford in Surrey, to begin her SOE training; and from there she went to Aylesbury, in Buckinghamshire, for special training as a wireless operator in occupied territory. Noor was the first woman to be sent to France as a wireless operator, since all of the women agents before her had been sent as couriers. Because of her previous wireless transmission training, she had an advantage over others who were just beginning their radio training. She was also both fast and accurate. It was while she was training that she adopted the name 'Nora Baker'.

From Aylesbury, Noor went to Beaulieu, in Hampshire, to try for a practice mission. Wireless operators had to find somewhere in a strange city from where they could transmit to their instructors, without being detected by an unknown agent, who would be shadowing them. The climax to the practice session was a mock Gestapo interrogation. This was supposed to show the agents what might happen to them if they were captured, and to give them practice in maintaining their cover story.

Noor's escorting officer found her mock interrogation 'almost unbearable' and reported that 'she seemed absolutely terrified... so overwhelmed she nearly lost her voice' and that afterwards, 'she was trembling and quite blanched'. The final report of Noor's training, which the official historian of F Section found in her personal file long after the war, read 'Not overburdened with brains but has worked hard and shown keenness, apart from some dislike of the security side of the course. She has an unstable and temperamental personality, and it is very doubtful whether she is really suited to the work in the field.' Next to this comment Maurice Buckmaster wrote in the margin, 'Nonsense'.

Noor had not finished training, but her fluency in French and the fact that she was the most competent wireless operator at that point, led to the decision to send her into Nazi–occupied France. The service was desperate for more radio operators in the field, particularly as the German occupation was becoming more intense. Noor was given the code name Madeleine and the cover identity of Jeanne-Marie Regnier, a children's nanny; and on the night of 16/17 June 1943, she was flown in a Lysander to a meadow a few miles north-east of Angers, in the Loire valley. She made her way to Paris and found the address given to her, where she made contact with Émile Henri Garry, who was to become Noor's network organiser. With two other women, Diana Rowden and Cécily Lefort, Noor joined the network, named 'Physician', which was led by Francis Suttill, whose code name was Prosper.

Noor had been in Paris for barely a week when three agents of the 'Physician' network were arrested by the *Sicherheitsdienst* (SD), the secret police.[7] Over the next six weeks, all the other radio operators in the 'Physician' network were also arrested. As the network collapsed, Noor moved between safe houses in Paris, managing to outwit the Gestapo, several times just managing to elude them, and transmit her messages with amazing speed and accuracy. Leo Marks noted that 'her transmissions were flawless, with all their security checks intact'. Despite the dangerous situation, Noor refused to return to Britain, as she realised the importance of contining transmissions between London and Paris, she being the last vital link.

Noor managed to elude the Gestapo throughout the summer and early autumn. She told some friends at the end of September, she would be going back to England very soon. However, in early October, the Gestapo was contacted by Renée Garry, Émile's sister, offering to sell them 'Madeleine', whom they knew was the F Section radio operator they had been unable to capture. Renée was allegedly paid 100,000 francs, much less than the Gestapo were prepared to pay for Noor. It's thought that Renée in fact betrayed Noor out of jealousy since she believed that Noor had 'stolen' her lover, SOE agent France Antelme. Renée gave the Gestapo Noor's address. Noor returned home on 13 October 1943, or thereabouts, to find a single Gestapo officer waiting for her, and she fought so ferociously that he had to cover her with his gun whilst he phoned for assistance. From her arrest onwards, she was categorised as highly dangerous.

Noor had always carried her notebook wherever she went. In it she had kept a record of all the messages she had sent and received since her arrival in France, both in code and in plain text. This seems to have arisen from her misunderstanding the phrase in her operational orders, 'be extremely careful with the filing of your messages'. She seemed to be unaware that 'filing' meant 'sending', and she thought she was supposed to keep them in a filing system. This was clearly a breathtakingly dangerous breach of the most elementary security precautions. The giveaway notebook with all her messages, codes and security checks was on her bedside table when she was arrested. The Gestapo also found her transmitter.

Noor was taken to the SD headquarters at 84 Avenue Foch in Paris. On arrival, she climbed out of a bathroom window onto a ledge attempting to escape. However, she was spotted and brought back in. For the next five weeks she was interrogated daily but there is no evidence that she was tortured. Despite being under increasing pressure to cooperate, Noor repeatedly told the Gestapo only that her name was Nora Baker and that she was a WAAF officer. The Gestapo had enough information from Noor's records to be able to send radio transmissions to London, the 'radio game'. Sadly, SOE didn't check the inconsistencies which would have warned them she was under enemy control. Because of this, when three more agents were sent to France, they were caught when they landed. Among them was Madeleine Damerment / Solange who was later executed. Noor had even sent a previously-agreed 18-letter signal intended to alert SOE to her arrest which they failed to spot.

Noor attempted to escape a second time on 25 November, with John Renshaw Starr and Leon Faye, also SOE agents, by loosening and removing the window bars. By sheer bad luck, there was an RAF air raid alert as they were escaping across the roof. Because the regulations demanded a headcount of prisoners, their escape was discovered before they could get away. Noor refused to sign a statement that she would make no further attempts to escape, so she was sent to the women's section of the civil prison at Pforzheim, Germany on 27 November 1943. Classed as 'highly dangerous', Noor's hands and feet were shackled in chains, and she was unable to feed or clean herself. For ten months, she was kept in complete isolation, in solitary confinement as a *Nacht und Nebel* ('Night and Fog') prisoner, separated from the rest of the prison by two sets of iron gates. The governor of the prison, interviewed after the war, stated that Noor was uncooperative and refused to give any information about her work or her fellow agents. He thought her 'tranquillity [solitary confinement] did her good'.

On 11 September 1944, Noor was taken to Karlsruhe and from there, along with three other F Section agents, Yolande Beekman, Elaine Plewman and Madeleine Damerment, to Dachau concentration camp, near Munich. In the early hours of the morning, 13 September 1944, the four women, kneeling in pairs and holding hands, were executed by a shot to the back of the head. Their bodies were immediately incinerated in the furnaces. In 1958, an anonymous Dutch prisoner stated that Noor had been kicked into a 'bloody mess' on the stone floor prior to her execution, by the high-ranking SS officer in charge of executions, Wilhelm Ruppertand. She died with the word *liberté* on her lips.

After the war, the head of Gestapo headquarters in Paris, Hans Josef Kieffer, was interrogated by Vera Atkins, Maurice Buckmaster's deputy. When she described Noor's death in Dachau, Kieffer broke down in tears.

Noor was posthumously awarded a British Mention in Dispatches and a French *Croix de Guerre avec etoile*. She was also awarded the George Cross in April 1949. The Citation read:

The KING has been graciously pleased to approve the posthumous award of the GEORGE CROSS to:—

Assistant Section Officer Nora INAYAT-KHAN (9901), Women's Auxiliary Air Force.

Assistant Section Officer Nora INAYAT-KHAN was the first woman operator to be infiltrated into enemy occupied France, and was landed by Lysander aircraft on 16th June, 1943. During the weeks immediately following her arrival, the Gestapo made mass arrests in the Paris Resistance groups to which she had been detailed. She refused however to abandon what had become the principal and most dangerous post in France, although given the opportunity to return to England, because she did not wish to leave her French comrades without communications and she hoped also to rebuild her group. She remained at her post therefore and did the excellent work which earned her a posthumous Mention in Despatches.

The Gestapo had a full description of her, but knew only her code name 'Madeleine'. They deployed considerable forces in their effort to catch her and so break the last remaining link with London. After three months she was betrayed to the Gestapo and taken to their HQ in the Avenue Foch. The Gestapo had found her codes and messages and were now in a position to work back to London. They asked her to cooperate, but she refused and gave them no information of any kind. She was imprisoned in one of the cells on the 5th floor of the Gestapo HQ and remained there for several weeks during which time she made two unsuccessful attempts at escape. She was asked to sign a declaration that she would make no further attempts but she refused and the Chief of the Gestapo obtained permission from Berlin to send her to Germany for 'safe custody'. She was the first agent to be sent to Germany.

Assistant Section Officer INAYAT-KHAN was sent to Karlsruhe in November, 1943, and then to Pforzheim where her cell was apart from the main prison. She was considered to be a particularly dangerous and uncooperative prisoner. The Director of the prison has also been interrogated and has confirmed that Assistant Section Officer INAYAT-KHAN, when interrogated by the Karlsruhe Gestapo, refused to give any information whatsoever, either as to her work or her colleagues.

She was taken with three others to Dachau Camp on the 12th September, 1944. On arrival, she was taken to the crematorium and shot.

Assistant Section Officer INAYAT-KHAN displayed the most conspicuous courage, both moral and physical over a period of more than 12 months.

1 Muriel Byck was the daughter of French Jews Luba Besia (née Golinska) and Jacques Byck, who had both taken British nationality. She was born in London. For more information, see http://www.64-baker-street.org

2 Lilian Rolfe and her twin sister Helen Fedora Rolfe were the daughters of George Rolfe, a British chartered accountant working in Paris. For more information, see http://www.64-baker-street.org

3 Cecily Lefort was born in London of Scottish ancestry, and lived on the coast of Brittany, France, from the age of 24 with her French husband, Dr Alex Lefort. For more information, see http://www.64-baker-street.org

4 Solange was Madeleine Damerment. For more information see http://www.biography base.com/biography/Damerment_Madeleine.html

5 Some historians have questioned whether this happened. It has been suggested that the incident was fabricated by the SOE, to make Violette's story seem more adventurous, in face of criticism of the organisation and questions about its necessity.

6 For more information about Noor's father and Sufism, see http://www.om-guru.com/html/saints/khan.html

7 For more information about the SD, see http://en.wikipedia.org/wiki/ Sicherheitsdienst

9 *Nacht und Nebel* prisoners were held in the concentration camp at Natzweiler - Struthof, in Alsace. They were mostly resistance fighters whose families were not told of their imprisonment, i.e. they were made to dissapear into the night and the fog.

* Eileen Nearne was found in her Torquay flat several days after her death by natural causes on 2 September 2010. She had become a reclusive lady, and her SOE past was not known by her neighbours.